The Secret
of the Rosary

The Secret of the Rosary

BY
ST. LOUIS MARY GRIGNION
DE MONTFORT

WITH AN APPENDIX OF
THE NEW LUMINOUS MYSTERIES

Illustrated

CATHOLIC BOOK PUBLISHING CORP.
NEW JERSEY

NIHIL OBSTAT: James M. Cafone, M.A., S.T.D.
Censor Librorum

IMPRIMATUR: ✠ Most Rev. John J. Myers, J.C.D., D.D.
Archbishop of Newark

The Nihil Obstat and Imprimatur are official declarations that a book or pamphlet is free of doctrinal or moral error. No implication is contained therein that those who have granted the Nihil Obstat and Imprimatur agree with the contents, opinions or statements expressed.

This new translation of the original French work by St. Louis entitled, *Le Secret Admirable du Très Saint Rosaire,* has been made by Rev. John A. Otto.

(T-108)

ISBN 978-0-89942-108-7

5 6 7 8 9 10

CONTENTS

FOURTH DECADE

**Excellence of the Holy Rosary as Seen in the
Wonders That God Has Worked through It** . 113

METHODS OF SAYING THE MOST HOLY ROSARY

APPENDIX I

PREFACE

Louis Mary Grignion de Montfort was born to a poor family on January 21, 1673, at Montfort, France. He was educated at the Jesuit College in Rennes and was ordained there in 1700.

The young priest was assigned to a hospital at Poitiers and his much needed organization of the hospital staff caused great resentment, leading to his resignation. However, during his stay there he organized a group of women into the Congregation of the Daughters of Divine Wisdom.

For most of his life, Father Louis was a poor, wandering preacher with his few possessions (Bible, Breviary, and Notebooks) carried in a knapsack on his shoulder. Some considered that this was undignified, and he was forbidden to preach from time to time.

Eventually Father Louis went to Rome where Pope Clement XI appointed him a "missionary apostolic," and he spent the rest of his life preaching popular missions in Poitiers and Brittany.

The Saint had an emotional style that reaped permanent results in the restoration of churches, almsgiving, and spiritual revival. He composed verses and hymns, some still in use today, and promoted the practice of the Rosary. His greatest success is regarded as the reconciliation of many Calvinists at La Rochelle.

In 1715, Louis organized several priests and formed the Missionaries of the Company of

Jesus. The Saint also laid the foundation for a teaching order that came to be called Brothers of St. Gabriel. All three of his Congregations have spread his ideas and ideals to people today.

This holy man gave one the impression of having benefited from a baptismal rebirth in the Pauline manner. He had the Apostle's visceral repugnance to evil and charismatic openness to life in the Spirit. Those who knew him as a child and growing boy say that he was "seized" by the Virgin right from his Baptism, like Saint Paul by Christ. Mystic union with Mary was the "Divine milieu" of his spiritual life and his missionary apostolate.

This voyager, who traveled 16,000 miles on foot, seemed made for action, yet left a considerable body of writing, all of it penned with an eye to pastoral ministry. Among his 164 handwritten Canticles, totaling more than 20,000 lines, only 24 actually sing the praise of Mary. But her name appears in nearly all, invoked to promote conversion of life, spiritual practice, union with Christ, and perseverance.

His principal work is *True Devotion to the Blessed Virgin*, which has become a classic and been translated into fifty languages. Indeed, one can say that the principal Marian movements of the last century have arisen through meditation on this impassioned work.

His second classic work is the present *Secret of the Rosary*, which has guided thousands of

Catholics in the best way to recite this great prayer to Jesus and Mary. The Saint cites writers before him and also brings his own insights to bear on the richness of the prayers recited and the benefits from meditating on the Mysteries. He assures us that those who faithfully pray the Rosary advance rapidly in the faith, live perfectly, die peacefully, and rise surely to eternal life.

Worn out by his indefatigable labor and preaching for Christ, Father Louis died in 1716 at Saint-Laurent-sur-Sevre, France, and was canonized in 1947 by Pope Pius XII.

Pope John Paul II has held St. Louis up as a witness and teacher of a true Marian spirituality, which finds its whole basis in Christ: "I would like to recall, among the many witnesses and teachers of this spirituality, the figure of St. Louis Mary Grignion de Montfort, who proposes consecration to Christ through the hands of Mary, as an effective means for Christians to live faithfully their baptismal commitments" *(Mother of the Redeemer,* no. 48).

The Pope also cited St. Louis first in a list "of all the many Saints who discovered in the Rosary a genuine path to growth in holiness" and he called him "the author of an excellent work on the Rosary *[The Secret of the Rosary]" (The Rosary of the Virgin Mary,* no. 8).

INTRODUCTION
A WHITE ROSE
For Priests

[1] MINISTERS of the Most High, preachers of the Truth, trumpets of the Gospel, let me give you this little book as a white rose. The truths contained in it are set forth in a very simple and direct manner. Put them in your heart and on your lips.

In your heart, so that you yourselves may make a practice of saying the Rosary and tasting its fruits. On your lips, so that you may preach to others the excellence of this holy practice and by your preaching convert them.

Beware, if you please, of looking upon this practice as trivial and meaningless—as do ignorant people and even some who are learned but proud. The Rosary is not a trivial thing. It is truly great, sublime, and inspired by God.

Almighty God has given it to you for converting the most hardened sinners, and the most obstinate heretics. God has attached grace to it in this life and glory in the next. Saints have prayed it, and Popes have endorsed it.

How blessed is the priest and director of souls to whom the Holy Spirit has made known the secret of the Rosary, its fruit-bearing potential. Most people know it not at all or only superficially. If such a priest really understands what the Rosary can do, he will pray it every day and encourage others to pray it. God and His Holy Mother will pour abundant grace into his soul and make him an instrument for God's glory. By his preaching, though simple, he will bear more fruit in one month than that of other preachers in years.

[2] Let us not be content, dear brother priests, with counseling others to pray the Holy Rosary. We must pray it ourselves. Even if we are convinced of the excellence of the Holy Rosary but never practice it, we can hardly expect people to accept our counsel to pray it. For no one can give what he does not have. "Jesus began to do and to teach" (Acts 1:1).

Let us imitate Jesus Christ, Who began by practicing what He preached. Let us imitate the Apostle, who knew and preached nothing but Jesus Christ crucified. You also will be preaching Jesus if you preach the Holy Rosary. For the Rosary is not, as we shall see, just a putting together of Our Fathers and Hail Marys but a Divine summary of the Mysteries of the Life, Passion, Death, and Glory of Jesus and Mary.

God has let me experience the effectiveness of preaching the Holy Rosary in the conversion of souls. If I thought that my experience could move you to preach the Holy Rosary in spite of the fact that this is not the custom, what would I do?

I would tell you about the wonderful conversions I have seen when preaching this holy devotion. But I am content with relating to you in this summary some earlier and well-received accounts about the Rosary. I have only, for your benefit, inserted some passages from good authors. These passages show what I set forth to the people.

A RED ROSE
For Sinners

[3] To you, poor men and women who are sinners, I, a greater sinner than you, offer this rose reddened by the Blood of Jesus Christ. I offer it that it may blossom and save you.

Ungodly people and unrepentant sinners cry daily: "Let us crown ourselves with roses" (Wisdom 2:8). We also cry: "Let us crown ourselves with roses of the Holy Rosary."

Their roses are far different from ours. Theirs are their pleasures of the flesh, their empty honors, and their perishable riches that soon wilt and rot away.

Ours are the Our Father and the Hail Mary said devoutly over and over as well as the good works we have done and the penitential acts we have made. These will never wilt or fade. Their brightness will be as radiant thousands of years from now as it is at present.

Sinners' roses only look like roses. In reality, they are thorns that prick them during life by giving them pangs of conscience. At their death, they pierce them with regret, and in eternity they burn them forever with rage and despair.

If our roses have thorns, they are the thorns of Jesus Christ, Who changes them into roses. If our roses prick, it is only for a time—and only to cure us of sin and save us.

[4] Let us crown ourselves in emulation of the roses of heaven and pray the entire Rosary every day, the fifteen decades or three Rosaries of five decades each. There are two reasons for praying all fifteen every day.

The first reason is to honor the three crowns of Jesus and Mary—Jesus' crown of grace in His Incarnation, His crown of thorns in His Passion, and His crown of glory in heaven, and the three-fold crown of Mary received in heaven from the Most Blessed Trinity.

The second reason is to receive three crowns from Jesus and Mary—a crown of merit in our lifetime, a crown of peace at our death, and a crown of glory in heaven.

If you are faithful in praying the Rosary devoutly until death, believe me that in spite of the gravity of your sins "you will receive an unfading crown of glory" (1 Peter 5:4).

Even if you are on the verge of being damned, even if you have one foot in hell, even if you have sold your soul to the devil as sorcerers do, even if you are a heretic as hardened and obstinate as a devil, sooner or later you will be converted and saved, if—mark well my words—if you pray the Holy Rosary devoutly every day until death for the purpose of knowing the truth and obtaining contrition and forgiveness for your sins.

In this little book you will find several accounts of great sinners who were converted by the power of the Holy Rosary. Read and meditate upon them.

God alone.

A MYSTICAL ROSE TREE
For Devout Souls

[5] KIND and devout souls, who share in the light of the Holy Spirit, do not mind that I am giving you this little mystical rose tree. It comes from heaven and is to be planted in the garden of your soul. It will not harm the sweet smelling flowers of your contemplations, because it is a heavenly tree and gives off a pleasant fragrance.

This little rose tree will not in the least spoil the order of your flower bed. Being itself very pure and very well-ordered, it makes everything tend toward purity and order. If watered and properly cared for every day, it will grow to a marvelous height and have a wonderful extent. It will not hinder your other devotions but further their growth and make them better.

You who are spiritually minded, understand my meaning. This mystical rose tree is Jesus and Mary in life, in death, and in eternity.

[6] Its green leaves denote the Joyful Mysteries of Jesus and Mary; the thorns, their Sorrowful Mysteries; and the flowers, their Glorious Mysteries. The rosebuds are the childhood of Jesus and Mary. The open roses represent them in their sufferings, and the roses in full bloom point to their triumph and glory.

A rose delights us by its beauty—so here are Jesus and Mary in their Joyful Mysteries. Its thorns are sharp and they prick, calling to mind Jesus and Mary in their Sorrowful Mysteries. Its fragrance is so sweet that it stands for them in their Glorious Mysteries.

Do not scorn this delightful and heavenly tree. Plant it yourselves in the garden of your soul, and make the resolution to say your Rosary every day. By saying it daily and doing good works you will be tending your tree and watering it.

In time you will see this Rosary bead, which now seems so small, become a tree large enough for the birds of the air—i.e., predestinate and contemplative souls—to build their nests in it and dwell there. The shade of its leaves will protect them from the heat of the sun. The height will keep them safe from the wild beasts on the ground. Best of all, they will feed upon the tree's fruit, which is none other than the adorable Jesus. To Him be honor and glory forever and ever. Amen. So be it.

God alone.

A ROSEBUD
For Little Children

[7] DEAR little friends, this beautiful rosebud is for you; it is one of the beads of your Rosary, and it may seem to you to be a tiny thing. If you only knew how precious this bead is! This wonderful bud will open out into a brilliantly colored rose if you say your Hail Mary devoutly.

It would be too much to ask you to say the whole fifteen Mysteries every day. Do say at least five Mysteries, and say them with love and devotion. This Rosary of five Mysteries will be your little wreath of roses, your crown for Jesus and Mary.

Remember what I have said and listen carefully to a true story I want to tell you and would like you to remember.

[8] Two little girls, two sisters, were saying the Rosary devoutly in front of their home. A beautiful Lady appeared, walked toward the younger of the

two—she was only about six or seven—took her by the hand, and led her away. Her older sister was startled and looked for the little girl but could not find her. So she went home and sorrowfully told her parents that someone had carried off her sister.

For three whole days the father and mother searched for their child without success. At the end of the third day they found her at the front door looking very happy and pleased.

They asked her where she had been, and she told them that the Lady to whom she had been saying her Rosary had taken her to a lovely place and given her delicious things to eat. She said that the Lady had also given her a Baby Boy to hold, and that He was very beautiful, and that she had kissed Him over and over.

The father and mother had been converted to the Catholic Faith only a short time before. They sent for the Jesuit priest who had instructed them in the Faith and had also taught them devotion to the Holy Rosary. They told him what had happened, and it was from this priest that we came to know the story you have just heard. It all took place in Paraguay.

So, my little children, imitate these little girls and say your Rosary every day, as they did. If you do so, you will be deserving of going to heaven and seeing Jesus and Mary. If they do not wish you to see them in this life, at least after you die you will see them for all eternity. Amen.

So let everyone— the learned and the ignorant, the righteous and the wicked, the great and the lowly—praise and greet Jesus and Mary, day and night, by saying the Holy Rosary. "My greetings to Mary, who has worked hard for you" (Romans 16:6).

FIRST DECADE

Excellence of the Holy Rosary in Its Origin and Name

FIRST ROSE
The Prayers of the Rosary

[9] THE Rosary is made up of two things: mental prayer and vocal prayer. The mental prayer of the Holy Rosary is the meditation on the principal Mysteries of the Life, Death, and Glory of Jesus Christ and His Most Holy Mother.

The vocal prayer of the Rosary consists in saying fifteen decades of the Hail Mary, each decade being headed by an Our Father, while at the same time we meditate on and contemplate the fifteen principal virtues that Jesus and Mary practiced in the fifteen Mysteries of the Holy Rosary.

In the first five decades we honor and meditate on the Joyful Mysteries; in the second five decades, the Sorrowful Mysteries; in the third five decades, the Glorious Mysteries.*

So the Rosary is a holy composite of mental and vocal prayer. By it we honor and learn to imitate the Mysteries and virtues of the Life, Passion and Death, and Glory of Jesus and Mary.

---

* See Appendix II, p. 229, for the new Luminous Mysteries.

SECOND ROSE

Origin of the Rosary

[10] SINCE the Holy Rosary is composed, essentially and substantially, of the Prayer of Christ and the Angelic Salutation—i.e., the Our Father and the Hail Mary—and of meditation on the Mysteries of Jesus and Mary, it was without doubt the first prayer and the principal devotion of the faithful. It has been in use through the centuries, from the time of the Apostles and the Disciples down to the present.

[11] But not until the year 1214 did the Church receive the Holy Rosary in the form and with the method according to which we pray it today. It was given to the Church by St. Dominic, who had received it from the Blessed Virgin as a means of converting the Albigensian heretics and sinners.

The Account of St. Dominic receiving the Rosary is found in a book by Blessed Alan de la Roche.*

Seeing that the gravity of the people's sins was hindering the conversion of the Albigensians, St. Dominic withdrew to a forest near Toulouse. There he prayed unceasingly for three days and three nights, weeping and performing harsh penances in order to appease God's anger. Throughout this time he flogged himself so much that his body was lacerated, and ultimately he fell into a coma.

---

* *On the Dignity of the Psalter of the Blessed Virgin,* i.e., the Holy Rosary. Blessed Alan was a French Dominican priest and apostle of the Holy Rosary.

At this point, the Blessed Virgin appeared to him, accompanied by three Angels of heaven, and she said:

"My dear Dominic, do you know which weapon the Blessed Trinity has used to reform the world?"

"My Lady," replied St. Dominic, "you know better than I because next to your Son Jesus Christ you were the chief instrument of our salvation."

Our Lady added: "I want you to know that the principal means has been the Angelic Psalter, which is the foundation of the New Testament. That is why, if you want to win these hardened hearts for God, preach my Psalter."

The Saint arose, comforted. Filled with zeal for the conversion of the Albigensians, he went straight to the cathedral church. Immediately, unseen Angels rang the bells to call to the church the inhabitants of Toulouse, and St. Dominic began to preach.

At the beginning of his sermon a frightful storm broke out. The earth shook, the sun became dim, and the thunder and lightning rendered his listeners pale and trembling. Their fright intensified when they glanced at an image of the Blessed Virgin, exposed in a prominent place, and saw her raise her arms to heaven three times to call down God's vengeance upon the people of Toulouse if they failed to be converted and seek the protection of the Holy Mother of God.

By means of these extraordinary happenings, God wanted to spread the new devotion of the Holy Rosary and make it more widely known.

At last, the storm came to an end in response to St. Dominic's prayers. He went on with his sermon and explained the value of the Holy Rosary so fervently and effectively that almost all the people of Toulouse embraced it and renounced their wrong beliefs. In a very short time, a great change was seen in the city: people renounced their bad habits and began living truly Christian lives.

THIRD ROSE
The Rosary and St. Dominic

[12] THE way the devotion of the Holy Rosary was given to us is somewhat similar to the way God gave His Law to the world on Mount Sinai and shows the great value of this sublime devotion.

Inspired by the Holy Spirit and instructed by the Blessed Virgin and his own experience, St. Dominic preached the Holy Rosary for the rest of his life. He preached it by example and by word of mouth, in cities and country places, before the great and the lowly, before the learned and the ignorant, before Catholics and heretics.

The Holy Rosary, which he said every day, was his preparation before preaching and his private meeting with our Lady afterward.

[13] One day he was to preach at the church of Notre Dame in Paris on the feast of St. John the Evangelist. He was in a little chapel behind the altar

preparing to preach by saying the Holy Rosary. The Blessed Virgin appeared to him and said:

"Dominic, although what you have prepared to preach is good, I am bringing you a much better sermon."

St. Dominic received from her hands a book that contained the sermon. He read the sermon, liked it, made it his own, and then gave thanks to the Blessed Virgin.

When the time came for the sermon, he went up into the pulpit and made no mention of St. John the Evangelist other than to say he had been found worthy to be the guardian of the Queen of Heaven. The illustrious assembly made up of theologians and other eminent people who had come to hear him were used to hearing exceptional and polished discourses. St. Dominic said he was not going to speak to them in the learned words of human wisdom but in the simplicity and power of the Holy Spirit.

Then the Saint preached the Holy Rosary to them and explained the Hail Mary, word by word, as to children. He used very simple illustrations, which he had found in the book the Blessed Virgin gave him.

[14] This fact has been taken from the book by Blessed Alan de la Roche *On the Dignity of the Psalter* (as reported by the great scholar Carthagena).

Blessed Alan states that Dominic appeared to him in a vision and said: "My son, you preach, and that is good; but so that you may not look for human praise rather than the salvation of souls, listen to what happened to me in Paris.

"I was to preach in the large church dedicated to the Blessed Virgin Mary and I wanted to speak in a cultivated manner. It was not pride that motivated me but consideration for the high intellectual capacity of those present.

"An hour before my sermon, I was praying my Rosary—as I always did before preaching—and fell into an ecstasy. I saw my friend, the Mother of God, bringing me a little book. 'Dominic,' she said, 'the sermon you have decided to preach is good, but I have brought you one that is much better.'

"Overjoyed, I took the book and read it through. Just as the Mother of God had said, I found exactly what I needed to say and thanked her with all my heart.

"When the time came for the sermon, I had before me the whole University of Paris and a large number of noblemen. They had heard of and seen the great signs the Lord was working through me.

"I went up into the pulpit. It was the feast of St. John, but of this Apostle I was content with saying only that he had been found worthy to be chosen guardian of the Queen of Heaven.

"Then I spoke to my audience as follows: 'Illustrious Lords and Masters at the University, you are accustomed to hearing elegant and learned sermons. However, now I do not want to address to you the scholarly words of human wisdom. On the contrary, I want to show you the Spirit of God and the Spirit's power.' "

Then Carthagena goes on to say—always in dependence on Blessed Alan—that St. Dominic went on to explain the Angelic Salutation to his audience using comparisons and examples familiar to them.

[15] The aforesaid Blessed Alan—as indicated by Carthagena—mentioned several other times when our Lord and the Blessed Virgin appeared to St. Dominic to urge and inspire him even more to preach the Holy Rosary increasingly for the purpose of destroying sin and converting sinners and heretics.

In one place, Carthagena writes: "Blessed Alan also said the Holy Virgin revealed to him that after she had appeared to St. Dominic, her Blessed Son appeared to him and said:

"Dominic, I rejoice to see that you are not relying on your own wisdom and are working with humility for the salvation of souls, rather than seeking to please conceited people.

"But many preachers want to thunder against the most grievous sins at the very outset, not realizing that before giving a bitter medicine to a sick person, we must make him ready to receive it and benefit by it.

"This is why preachers should first exhort their listeners to love prayer and especially to love my Angelic Psalter. If all the listeners began to pray my Angelic Psalter, there is no doubt that God in His clemency would be propitious to the ones who persevered. Therefore, preach my Rosary."

[16] In another place Blessed Alan says:

"All Christian preachers begin their sermons by asking the faithful to say a Hail Mary with the intention of obtaining God's grace. They do so because of a revelation made to St. Dominic by the Blessed Virgin.

" 'My son,' she said, 'do not be surprised at the lack of success in your preaching. You are trying to plow a ground that has not been watered by rain. Mark that when God wanted to renew the world, he first sent the rain of the Angelic Salutation. That is how the world was made new.

" 'In your sermons, therefore, exhort people to pray my Rosary, and you will reap much fruit for souls.' This St. Dominic steadfastly did, and then his preaching had remarkable success." *

[17] I have taken leave to cite word for word these passages (translated from the Latin) of well-known authors for the benefit of preachers and learned persons who might have doubts about the wonderful power of the Holy Rosary.

So long as priests followed St. Dominic's example and preached devotion to the Holy Rosary, piety and fervor flourished in the religious orders that practiced this devotion and in the whole Christian world. But when people began to neglect this gift from heaven, sins and disturbances were seen everywhere.

---

* St. Louis adds: "This is found in *The Book of the Miracles of the Holy Rosary* written in Italian and in Sermon 143 of Justin." However, in reality these things are found in *Sermons on the Litany of Loreto by Justin Mieckovic* in Sermon 243.

FOURTH ROSE

The Rosary and Blessed Alan de la Roche

[18] ALL things, even the most holy, are subject to change, particularly things that depend on our free will. No wonder, then, that the Confraternity of the Holy Rosary retained its first fervor for only a hundred years or so after its institution. It almost became like something buried and forgotten.

Doubtless, too, the malice and envy of the devil helped to make people neglect the Holy Rosary. Their neglect brought a halt to the flow of God's grace—the grace that had been drawn down upon the world through the Holy Rosary.

As if in retribution Divine Justice, in 1349, afflicted all the kingdoms of Europe with the most dreadful plague that had ever been seen. From the East it spread to Italy, Germany, France, Poland, and Hungary. It laid waste almost all these lands and claimed the life of people in untold numbers. Out of a hundred, scarcely one survived.

Cities towns, villages, and monasteries were almost completely depopulated during the three years the plague lasted.

This scourge of God was followed by two others: the heresy of the Flagellants and, in 1376, a disastrous schism.

[19] When by the mercy of God these tribulations were over, the Holy Virgin told Blessed Alan de la Roche—an eminent theologian and famous preacher of the Order of St. Dominic—to revive the

moribund Confraternity of the Holy Rosary. He was from the monastery of Dinan in the province of Brittany, and since the Confraternity had its beginning there, it was fitting that a Dominican from the same province should have the honor of reviving it.

Blessed Alan began this great work in 1460—as he himself says—after our Lord Jesus Christ, Who wanted to prompt him to preach the Rosary, spoke to him in the Sacred Host while he was celebrating Mass. "Why are you crucifying Me again so soon?" said Jesus.

"What are You saying, Lord?" asked Blessed Alan, greatly shocked.

"Yes, it was your sins that crucified Me once before," replied Jesus, "and I would rather be crucified again than see My Father offended by the sins you used to commit.

"And even now you are crucifying Me because you have the knowledge and ability to preach My Mother's Rosary, but you are not doing so. By means of the Rosary you could teach many souls and draw them away from sin, thus saving them and keeping them away from great evils; but you are not doing it, and so you are guilty of the sins they commit."

These severe reproaches made Blessed Alan resolve to preach the Rosary unceasingly.*

[20] The Blessed Virgin also spoke to him one day to inspire him to preach the Rosary more and more:

---

* See Alan de la Roche, *On the Dignity of the Psalter*, ch. 9.

"You were a great sinner in your youth, but I have obtained from my Son your conversion. I have prayed for you and, had it been possible, I would have desired to go through all kinds of suffering to save you because converted sinners are my glory. I would also have done this to make you worthy of preaching my Rosary everywhere."

St. Dominic, too, appeared to Blessed Alan and told him of the great results he had among the people through this beautiful devotion that he was preaching to them continually. He said to Blessed Alan:

"You see the results I have had from preaching the Holy Rosary. Do as I have done—you and all others who love our Lady—so that by this holy practice of the Rosary you may draw all people to true knowledge of the virtues."*

This in brief is what history teaches us about the institution of the Holy Rosary by St. Dominic and its revival by Blessed Alan de la Roche.

FIFTH ROSE

Confraternity of the Rosary

[21]   Properly speaking, there is only one kind of Confraternity of the Rosary—one composed of 150 Hail Marys. But in relation to people who practice this devotion, there are three kinds: that of the com-

---

* Alan de la Roche, *Ibid.*, ch. 13.

mon or ordinary Rosary, that of the perpetual Rosary, and that of the daily Rosary.

The Confraternity of the *ordinary* Rosary requires saying it once a week; that of the *perpetual* Rosary, entails saying it once a year; and that of the *daily* Rosary calls for saying it every day in its entirety, i.e., 150 Hail Marys.

None of these Rosaries binds under pain of sin, not even venial, because this commitment is completely voluntary and over and above what is expected.

Nonetheless, people should not join the Confraternity unless they intend to pray the Rosary in the way the Confraternity requires and as often as they can without neglecting the duties of their state in life.

If there is a conflict between a duty of one's state in life and the Rosary, holy as the Rosary is, one must give preference to the duty.

Likewise, sick people are not obliged to pray the whole Rosary or even part of it if doing so would make their illness worse.

If you cannot pray the Rosary because of a duty required by legitimate obedience, or because you really forgot or are facing an urgent necessity, there is no sin, not even venial. You do not even lose your share in the graces and merits of the other brothers and sisters of the Holy Rosary who are praying it throughout the world.

My dear Catholic people, even if you fail to pray the Rosary out of sheer neglect but without any formal contempt for it, you do not sin, absolutely speaking—but you lose your share in the prayers, good works, and merits of the Confraternity. Moreover, because you have not been faithful in things that are little and freely chosen, you will fall, without noticing it, into neglect of big things that bind under pain of sin. For "anyone who looks down on little things will fall by little and little" (Sirach 19:1).*

SIXTH ROSE
Mary's Psalter

[22] FROM the time St. Dominic established the devotion of the Holy Rosary and Blessed Alan de la Roche reestablished it in 1460 by command from heaven, the Rosary has been called the Psalter of Jesus and Mary. The reason is that it has as many Hail Marys as the Psalter of David has Psalms.

Simple and unlettered people could not say the Psalter of David. They found instead in the saying of the Rosary a fruit equal to the fruit other people drew from saying the Psalms of David. Indeed, the Rosary can be regarded as even more beneficial than the latter for the following reasons:

(1) The Angelic Psalter has a nobler fruit, the Word Incarnate, whereas David's Psalter only prophesies Him.

---

*Throughout this discussion membership in the Confraternity is presupposed.

(2) Just as the truth surpasses the figure and the body the shadow, so the Psalter of our Lady surpasses the Psalter of David, which was only its shadow and figure.

(3) The Holy Trinity directly made the Psalter of our Lady, i.e., the Rosary composed of the Our Father and Hail Mary.*

[23] The Psalter or Rosary of our Lady is divided into three chaplets of five decades each, for the following purposes:

(1) To honor the three Persons of the Holy Trinity.

(2) To honor the Life, Death, and Glory of Jesus Christ.

(3) To imitate the Church Triumphant, to help the Church Militant, and to comfort the Church Suffering.

(4) To imitate the three parts of the Psalter:

(a) the first being for the purgative life,

---

* Here is what the learned Carthagena has to say in regard to this matter:

"The very noted writer of Aix-La-Chapelle (J. Beyssel) says in his book *The Crown of Roses* dedicated to Emperor Maxmillian: 'It cannot be sustained that the Marian Salutation is a recent invention. In fact, it originated and spread with the Church herself.

" 'For at the very beginnings of the Church, the more learned faithful assiduously celebrated the praise of God with the 150 psalms of David. Among the most simple, who encountered difficulty in the Divine Office, there arose a holy emulation. . . .

" 'They rightly considered that the heavenly praises of the Rosary contained all the Divine Mysteries of the Psalms. For while the Psalms sing of the One Who was to come, the Rosary is addressed to Him as having already come.

" 'Hence, they applied the name "The Psalter of Mary" to the 150 Salutations and preceded each decade with an Our Father as they had seen done by those who recited the Psalms' " (*De Sacris Arcanis*, bk. 12, hom. 1).

(b) the second for the illuminative life,

(c) and the third for the unitive life.

(5) To fill us with graces during life, peace at death, and glory in eternity.

SEVENTH ROSE

The Rosary, Crown of Roses

[24] From the time that Blessed Alan de la Roche renewed this devotion, the voice of the people, which is the voice of God, has given it the name "Rosary," i.e., "Crown of Roses." Every time, then, that people pray the Rosary they place upon the heads of Jesus and Mary a crown of 153 white roses and 16 red roses from heaven. These roses will never lose their beauty or their brightness.

Our Lady showed her approval of the name Rosary. She made known to several people that each time they said the Hail Mary in her honor they were giving her a pleasing rose, and each time they said the Rosary they were giving her a crown of roses.

[25] Brother Alphonsus Rodriguez, of the Company of Jesus, used to say his Rosary so devoutly that he often saw a red rose come out of his mouth at each Our Father and a white rose at each Hail Mary. The roses were equal in beauty and fragrance, and only different in color.

The Chronicles of St. Francis tell of a young friar who had the praiseworthy habit of saying this Crown of our Lady every day before the noon meal. One day for some unknown reason he failed to say it. When the refectory bell rang, he asked the Superior to allow him to say it before coming to the table. With this permission, he went to his room; but because he stayed there too long, the Superior sent a friar to call him.

This friar found him in his room. He was bathed in a heavenly light with our Lady and two Angels by his side. Every time he said a Hail Mary a beautiful rose came out of his mouth. The Angels took the roses one by one and placed them on our Lady's head, who smiled and accepted them.

Two other friars sent to find out what caused the delay of the first two saw all this Mystery, for the Holy Virgin did not leave until the fifteen decades of the Rosary had been said.

The complete Rosary is a large crown of roses and the chaplet of decades is a little wreath of flowers or a small crown of heavenly roses that we place on the heads of Jesus and Mary. The rose is the queen of flowers. Similarly, the Rosary is the rose of devotions and therefore the principal devotion.

EIGHTH ROSE

Wonders of the Rosary

[26] OUR Lady's esteem for the Rosary can scarcely be put into words. She regards it more highly than all other devotions. She magnificently rewards those who preach the Rosary and go to great lengths to introduce and to spread it. On the other hand, she severely rebukes those who oppose its promotion.

St. Dominic had nothing more at heart in life than to praise our Lady, to preach her greatness, and to inspire everyone to honor her by saying her Rosary. In turn, the powerful Queen of Heaven showered blessings on this Saint. She crowned his labors with many miracles and prodigies. Through her intercession God always granted him what he asked. The highest favor was that she rendered him victorious over the Albigensian heresy and made him father and patriarch of a great religious Order.

[27] As for Blessed Alan de la Roche, who revived the devotion of the Rosary, of him it should be noted that our Lady honored him several times with her visit. She taught him how to work out his salvation and how to become a good priest, a perfect religious, and an imitator of Jesus Christ.

Devils used to tempt and persecute Blessed Alan most horribly, making him very sad and sometimes even bringing him close to despair. At such times, our Lady always comforted him with her sweet presence, which drove away the clouds of darkness that hung over his soul.

She taught him how to say the Rosary and explained its value and the fruits to be gained by it. She favored him with the glorious title of her new spouse and—as pledge of her chaste affection for him—she placed a ring on his finger and a necklace made of her own hair around his neck, and she gave him a crown of the Rosary.

The priest Tritème, the learned Carthagena, the scholarly Martin Navarre, and others spoke of him with high praise.

Blessed Alan died at Zunolle in Flanders, September 8, 1475, after having brought over 100,000 people into the Confraternity of the Rosary.

[28] Blessed Thomas of St. John was a well-known preacher of the Rosary. The devil, jealous of the results Blessed Thomas had from his preaching, inflicted such pain on him that he fell ill for a long time. The doctors declared that there was no hope of recovery. One night when Blessed Thomas thought he was surely going to die, the devil appeared to him in a most hideous form. Lifting his eyes and heart to a picture of our Lady near his bed, the Saint cried out with all his strength: "Help me, comfort me, O my most sweet Mother!" He had scarcely said this when the picture seemed to take on life. Our Lady stretched out her hand, took hold of his arm, and said:

"Do not be afraid, Thomas my son, I am here and I am going to help you. Get up and continue to preach devotion to my Rosary, as you have begun to do. I will defend you against all your enemies."

At these words of our Lady, the devil fled. Blessed Thomas got up and, finding himself in perfect health, gave thanks to his good Mother with tears of joy. He continued to preach the Rosary and had wonderful success.

[29] Our Lady not only blesses those who preach her Rosary; she also splendidly rewards those who by their example lead others to say it.

Alphonsus, King of Leon and Galicia, was very desirous that his servants should honor the Blessed Virgin by saying the Rosary. To induce them to do so by his example, he always wore a large Rosary on his belt though he never said it himself. In this way, he did encourage his court, servants included, to pray it devoutly.

The king fell seriously ill, and when he was at death's door he found himself, in a vision, before the judgment seat of Jesus Christ. He saw devils who were accusing him of all the sins he had committed. Our Lord as Judge was about to condemn him to eternal punishment when our Lady interceded for him with her Son.

She called for a pair of scales. On one side, she put all the sins of the king. On the other side, she put the large Rosary he had always worn in her honor, together with all the Rosaries that had been said because of his example. The Rosaries weighed more than all his sins.

Gazing lovingly at him, the Blessed Virgin said: "As a reward for the small service you rendered to me in wearing the Rosary, I have obtained from my Son a few more years of life for you. Use them well, and do penance."

On coming out of the vision, the king exclaimed: "Blessed be the Rosary of the holy Virgin, by which I have been delivered from eternal damnation." After regaining his health, he spent the rest of his life in spreading devotion to the Holy Rosary, and he prayed it every day.

Those devoted to the Blessed Virgin should follow the example of this king and of the Saints mentioned above and bring into the Confraternity of the Rosary as many of the faithful as they can. Such people will have great graces on earth and eternal life hereafter: "They that explain me shall have life everlasting" (Sirach 24:31).

NINTH ROSE
Enemies of the Rosary

[30] We see then what an injustice it is to hinder the progress of the Confraternity of the Rosary. Indeed, God has punished people who showed contempt for the Confraternity and sought to destroy it.

God has also given His approval to the devotion of the Rosary by means of numerous miracles, and the Church has approved it by means of countless papal bulls. Yet there are still libertines and free-thinkers who belittle the Confraternity of the

Rosary or at least strive to turn the faithful away from it.

It is easy to see that their tongues have been infected by the poison of hell and that they are influenced by the devil. For no one can disapprove of the devotion of the Holy Rosary without condemning what is most sacred in the Catholic Faith: i.e., the Lord's Prayer, the Angelic Salutation, and the Mysteries of the Life, Death, and Glory of Jesus Christ and His Holy Mother.

These freethinkers cannot tolerate the fact that people say the Rosary. Often they fall, insensibly, into the reprobate way of heretics who abhor the chaplet and the Rosary.

To abhor confraternities is to turn away from God and true piety, because our Lord assures us He is in the midst of people who are gathered together in His name.

It should also be said that a good Catholic does not neglect the many indulgences the Church has granted to confraternities.

Nor does a good Catholic turn the faithful away from the Confraternity of the Rosary. Anyone who does turn them away is an enemy of souls, because the Rosary helps people leave the path of sin and embrace piety.

St. Bonaventure says [in his *Psalter]* that he who neglects devotion to the Blessed Virgin will die in his sins and be damned. If such be the punishment for neglecting her, what must be the punishment in store for people who turn others away from devotion to her!

TENTH ROSE

Miracles Obtained through the Rosary

[31] WHEN St. Dominic was preaching the Rosary in Carcassone, a heretic poked fun at the miracles and the fifteen Mysteries of the Rosary. His ridicule hindered the conversion of heretics. As punishment God permitted fifteen thousand devils to possess the man.

His parents then brought him to Father Dominic to be freed from these malicious spirits. Father Dominic began to pray and asked everyone there to say the Rosary out loud with him. At each Hail Mary, our Lady drove one hundred devils out of this heretic's body, and they came out in the form of red hot coals.

After the man was freed from the malicious spirits, he renounced his errors, was converted, and joined the Confraternity of the Rosary. Several of his coreligionists did the same, having been greatly moved by his punishment and the power of the Rosary.

[32] The learned Carthagena of the Order of St. Francis, as well as several other authors, records the following event. In 1482, the Venerable James Sprenger and some other members of the Franciscan Order were working zealously to reestablish the devotion to the Rosary and to set up a Confraternity in Cologne.

Two well-known preachers became jealous of the great fruits Sprenger and his confreres were achieving by this practice. So they sought to discredit it by their sermons. Since they were talented and highly thought of, they succeeded in dissuading many people from joining the Confraternity.

One of these preachers, the better to gain his wicked end, prepared a special sermon against the Rosary and was going to give it the following Sunday. When the time came for the sermon, he never showed up.

After some waiting around, people went looking for him and found him dead. Apparently he had died all alone and no one had been there to help him.

The other preacher convinced himself that his friend's death had been due to natural causes. So he resolved to make up for his friend's absence by putting an end to the Confraternity of the Rosary. The day came for him to preach, and when it was time for the sermon God punished him with paralysis that left him without the use of his arms and legs and without his power of speech.

Finally acknowledging his error and that of his friend, he had recourse in his heart to the Blessed Virgin, promising her to preach the Rosary as forcefully as he had fought against it. To this end, he implored her to restore his health and speech, and the Blessed Virgin granted him his petition. Finding himself suddenly cured, he rose up like another Saul, turning from a persecutor into a defender of the Rosary. He made public reparation for his error and preached the excellence of the Holy Rosary with zeal and eloquence.

[33] I have no doubt that the freethinkers and critics of our day who read the narratives in this little book will question their authenticity, just as they have always done. Yet the narratives come from very good contemporary authors and, in part, from a book written a short time ago: *The Mystical Rose Tree,* by Father Antonin Thomas, O.P.

Everyone knows there are three different kinds of faith to be given to different kinds of narratives.

To narratives of Holy Scripture we owe *divine faith.*

To secular narratives that are not inconsistent with reason and are written by good authors, we owe *human faith.*

To pious narratives by good authors and not contrary to reason or faith and good morals, even though sometimes they deal with extraordinary matters, we owe *pious faith.*

I know we should be neither too credulous nor too critical and should hold the middle in all things to find the point of truth and virtue. But I also know that charity easily leads us to believe all that is not contrary to faith or good morals: "Charity believes all things" (1 Corinthians 13:7), whereas pride easily leads us to deny almost all well-authenticated narratives, on the pretext they are not in Holy Scripture.

Such pretext is one of the devil's snares. Heretics who deny Tradition have fallen into it, and critics of our time are falling into it unawares. These critics refuse to believe what they do not understand or what is not to their liking. They are motivated by pride and a distorted view of their own mind's sufficiency.

SECOND DECADE

Excellence of the Holy Rosary in the Prayers of Which It Is Composed

---

ELEVENTH ROSE
Excellence of the Creed

[34] THE Creed or the Symbol of the Apostles, which is said on the crucifix of the Rosary, is a holy summary of Christian truths. It is a prayer of great merit because faith is the base, the foundation, and the beginning of all Christian virtues, of all eternal truths, and of all prayers that are pleasing to God.

"He that comes to God must believe" (Hebrews 11:6). Whoever comes to God in prayer must begin by believing, and the greater his faith the more merit his prayer will have, the more meritorious it will be for him, and the more it will glorify God.

I cannot stop here to explain the Apostles' Creed, but I will say that the words "I believe in God" are marvelously effective as a means of sanctifying the soul and putting devils to rout, because these words contain the acts of the three theological virtues: faith, hope, and charity.

By saying *I believe in God* many Saints overcame temptations, especially temptations against faith, hope, and charity—whether they were tempted in the course of their life or at the time of their death. These words were also the last spoken by the Dominican St. Peter the Martyr.*

A heretic had split the holy martyr's skull in two by a blow of his sword. As St. Peter lay breathing his last, somehow he was able to write these words in the sand with his finger before he died.

[35] Faith is the single key to the understanding of all the Mysteries of Jesus and Mary contained in the Holy Rosary. That is why we begin it by reciting the Creed with great attention and devotion—and the stronger is our faith the more meritorious will be our Rosary.

This faith must be a living one that is filled with charity; in other words, to pray the Rosary profitably we must be in God's grace or at least in search of it.

It must also be a strong and unwavering faith, i.e., we should not be looking only for sensible delight or only for spiritual consolation in the recitation of the Rosary. Neither should we give it up because we are afflicted with streams of involuntary distractions or because we are experiencing a strange distaste in the soul and oppressive weariness in the body.

In order to say the Rosary well, we have no need of joy, consolation, sighs, ecstasies, or the continual

---

* St. Peter of Verona, O.P. (1206-1252) was a Dominican priest who had received the habit from St. Dominic himself. In 1234 he was appointed Inquisitor General for Lombardy by Pope Gregory IX. In carrying out the duties of his office to stamp out heresy, Peter was martyred. Before his death, he prayed for his attacker, a heretic named Carino, who later repented, abjured his heresy, became a Dominican laybrother, and died a holy death. Pope Innocent IV canonized Peter the Martyr in 1253.

use of the imagination. Pure faith and a good intention are enough. *Faith alone suffices.**

TWELFTH ROSE
Excellence of the Our Father

[36] THE Our Father or the Lord's Prayer derives all its excellence from its Author, Who is neither a man nor an Angel but the King of Angels and of men, our Lord and Savior Jesus Christ.

"It was necessary," says St. Cyprian, "that He Who came to give us the life of grace as our Savior should also teach us the way to pray as our heavenly Teacher."

The wisdom of this Divine Teacher appears in the order, the tenderness, the power, and the clarity of this Divine prayer. It is short but rich in instruction, within the grasp of the unlettered and filled with Mysteries for the learned.

The Our Father contains all our duties toward God, the acts of all the virtues, and the petitions for all our spiritual and corporal needs.

Tertullian says that the Our Father is "a summary of the Gospel."

Thomas à Kempis says that the Our Father "surpasses all the desires of the Saints" and is a concise statement of all the beautiful sayings of the Psalms and Canticles; it asks for everything we need, praises God in an excellent way, lifts up the soul from earth to heaven, and unites it with God.

---

* Words from the hymn *Pange Lingua* ("Sing My Tongue").

[37] St. John Chrysostom says we cannot be our Divine Teacher's disciples unless we pray as He did and as He taught us to pray. Indeed, God the Father listens more favorably to the Prayer His Son taught us than to prayers the human mind has composed.

We should pray the Our Father with the certainty that the eternal Father will hear it because it is the prayer of His Son, Whom He always hears, and because we are members of the Son. How could such a good Father refuse a request so duly conceived and supported by the merits and the recommendation of so worthy a Son?

St. Augustine assures us that the Our Father devoutly said takes away venial sins.

The righteous man falls seven times a day. The Lord's Prayer contains seven petitions by which we can remedy the falls and protect ourselves from spiritual enemies.

The Lord's Prayer is short and easy to say so that, since we are weak and prone to difficulties, we might say it more often and more devoutly and thus more quickly receive the help we need.

[38] Therefore, stop deceiving yourselves, you devout souls who neglect the Prayer God's own Son composed and asked us all to say. You only have regard for the prayers people have written, as if anyone, even the most intelligent, knew better how we ought to pray than the Lord Himself. You look in books written by people for the way to praise and to pray to God, as though you were ashamed to use the way His Son told us to use.

You think that the prayers in these books are for the learned and the wealthy whereas the Rosary is only for women and children and the poor, as though the praises and prayers you have been reading were more beautiful and pleasing to God than the prayers and praises to be found in the Lord's Prayer.

It is a very dangerous temptation to cast aside the Prayer our Lord recommended to us and instead make use of prayers written by people.

I do not disapprove of the prayers Saints have written to rouse the faithful to praise God, but it is intolerable that prayers of the Saints should be preferred to the Prayer that was uttered by Wisdom Incarnate. If the faithful disdain this Prayer, they are like people who pass up the spring to go after the brook and, refusing the clear water, drink dirty water instead.

Because the Rosary is made up of the Lord's Prayer and the Angelic Salutation, it is this clear and ever-flowing water that comes from the Fountain of Grace. Other prayers that people look for in books are only tiny streams that have their source in this Fountain.

[39] People who say the Lord's Prayer attentively, weighing every word, may indeed be called blessed. In it they find everything they need and everything they can desire.

When we say this wonderful prayer, we captivate God's heart by addressing Him with the sweet name of Father.

Our Father:

He is the most tender of fathers: all-powerful in His work of creation, all-wonderful in the way He maintains the world, all-lovable in His Providence, all-good and infinitely good in the Redemption.

God is our Father, we are all brothers and sisters, and heaven is our homeland and our heritage. This should more than suffice to inspire us with love of God, love of neighbor, and detachment from the things of the world.

Let us, then, love such a Father and say to Him thousands upon thousands of times:

Our Father, *Who art in heaven:*
You fill heaven and earth
by the immensity of Your Being.
You are present everywhere:
You are in the Saints by Your glory,
in the damned by Your justice,
in the righteous by Your grace,
in sinners by the patience with which You
tolerate them.
Grant, we beseech You,
that we may always be mindful of our heavenly origin.
Grant that we may live
as truly Your children.
Grant that we may always tend toward You alone
with all the ardor of our desires.

Hallowed be Thy name:

King David, the prophet, says the name of the Lord is holy and awesome. Isaiah says heaven echoes with the praises the Seraphim give unceasingly to the holiness of the Lord, God of hosts.

When we say *hallowed be Thy name,* we ask that all the world may know and adore the attributes of this God Who is so great and so holy. We ask that He may be known, loved, and adored by pagans, Turks, Jews, the uncivilized, and all unbelievers. We ask that all people may serve and glorify Him by a living faith, a steadfast hope, an ardent charity, and the renunciation of all erroneous beliefs. In a word, we pray that all people may be holy because God Himself is holy.

> *Thy kingdom come:*
> May You reign in our souls
> by Your grace during life,
> so that after death
> we may be found worthy
> to reign with You in Your kingdom.
> To reign with You
> is perfect and unending happiness.
> We believe in this happiness.
> We hope for and expect it
> because it is promised us by the Father.
> It was purchased for us
> by the merits of the Son
> and made known to us
> by the light of the Holy Spirit.

Thy will be done on earth as it is in heaven:
Nothing can escape the arrangements of Divine Providence, which foresaw everything and arranged everything before it happened. No

obstruction can divert Divine Providence from its purpose.

When we ask God that His will be done, it is not that we are afraid, says Tertullian, lest someone should actually prevent God's designs from being carried out.

Rather, when we say *Thy will be done,* we acquiesce in all it has pleased God to arrange as regards ourselves. We ask that we may always and in everything obey His most holy will, made known to us in His commandments, and obey it as promptly, lovingly, and faithfully as the Saints and the Angels do in heaven.

[40] *Give us this day our daily bread:*

Our Lord teaches us to ask God for everything we need for the life of the body and the life of the soul. With these words we humbly acknowledge our needs and pay honor to God. We say we believe all temporal blessings flow from His Providence.

When we say *bread,* we ask for the necessities of life: food, shelter, clothing. Luxuries are not included.

We ask for bread *this day,* which means our concern is only for the present. The future (tomorrow) we leave in the hands of Providence.

In asking for our *daily bread* we acknowledge that we have recurring needs and depend continually on God for His help and protection.

Forgive us our trespasses as we forgive those who trespass against us:

Our sins, say St. Augustine and Tertullian, are debts we owe to God, and His justice demands payment down to the last penny. Unhappily, we all have these sad debts.

No matter the number of our sins, we should go to God in all confidence and, with true repentance, say to Him:

"Our Father Who art in heaven, forgive us the sins of our heart and our mouth, the sins of commission and omission, all of which make us infinitely guilty in the eyes of Your justice.

"We ask this of You because You are a loving and merciful Father, and because out of obedience to You and out of charity we, Your children, forgive those who have done wrong to us.

And lead us not into temptation, but deliver us from evil:

"Do not let us, in spite of our unfaithfulness to Your graces, give in to the temptations of the world, the devil, and the flesh."

But deliver us from evil: i.e., the evil of sin but also the evil of temporal punishment and everlasting punishment, which we have deserved.

Amen (So be it):

This word at the end of the Our Father is very consoling. St. Jerome says that it is like a seal God puts at the end of our petitions to assure us He has heard us, as though He Himself were answering: "*Amen!* May it be as you have asked. You have

indeed obtained what you asked for." This is what
is meant by the word "Amen."

THIRTEENTH ROSE

Excellence of the Our Father (cont'd)

[41] EVERY word of the Lord's Prayer pays honor
to some perfection of God. The name *Father* honors
His fertility:

> Father,
> from all eternity
> You beget a Son,
> Who is God like You,
> Eternal, consubstantial with You.
> He is the same essence as You,
> and of the same power,
> the same goodness,
> and the same wisdom as You.
> Father and Son,
> by Your mutual love
> You produce the Holy Spirit,
> Who is God like You:
> Three Persons worthy of adoration,
> Who are but one God.

Our Father—This means He is the Father of us
all because He created us and keeps us in existence, and because He redeemed us. He is also the
merciful Father of sinners, the Father Who is the

friend of the righteous on earth and the glorious Father of the Blessed in heaven.

Who art—By these words we admire the infinity and immensity and fullness of God's essence. God is rightly called "He Who is" (Exodus 3:14); i.e., He exists necessarily, essentially, and eternally. He is the Being of beings, the Cause of all beings. He possesses, to an eminent degree, the perfection of all beings. He is in all of them by His essence, by His presence, and by His power without being limited by any of them.

We honor His greatness, His glory, and His majesty by the words *Who art in heaven*, seated as though on His throne dispensing justice to everyone.

When we say *hallowed be Thy name*, we worship God's holiness. We acknowledge His sovereignty and the justice of His laws when we say *Thy kingdom come* and we desire that people on earth obey Him as the Angels do in heaven.

We show our trust in God's Providence by asking Him for *our daily bread*, and we appeal to His mercy by asking Him to *forgive us our trespasses*. We have recourse to His power when we ask Him to *lead us not into temptation*, and we rely on His goodness when we hope He will *deliver us from evil*.

The Son of God always glorified His Father by His works, and He came into the world that the Father might be glorified by us. He taught us the way to honor the Father, namely, by the prayer He deigned to dictate to us Himself, the Lord's Prayer.

Therefore, we ought to say it often—with attention and in the spirit in which He composed it.

FOURTEENTH ROSE

Excellence of the Our Father (cont'd)

[42] Wʜᴇɴ we say this Divine Prayer attentively, we make as many acts of the noblest Christian virtues as we pronounce words.

In saying *Our Father Who art in heaven,* we make acts of faith, adoration, and humility. In wanting *His name to be hallowed* and glorified, we show an ardent zeal for His glory. In asking for *His kingdom to come,* we make an act of hope. By the wish that *His will be done on earth as it is in heaven,* we show a spirit of perfect obedience. In asking Him for our *daily bread,* we practice the spirit of poverty and detachment from the things of the world.

In beseeching Him to *forgive us our trespasses,* we make an act of repentance. By *forgiving those who have trespassed against us,* we show mercy in its highest perfection. In asking Him for His *help in temptations,* we make acts of humility, prudence, and fortitude. While waiting for Him to *deliver us from evil,* we practice patience.

Finally, in asking for all these things—not only for ourselves but also for our neighbor and all members of the Church—we are doing our duty as true children of God; we are imitating Him in His love, which embraces all people, and we are keeping the commandment of love of neighbor.

[43]   We detest all sins and obey all commands of God when, in saying the Lord's Prayer, our heart is in accord with our speech and we have no intentions contrary to the meaning of these Divine words. Whenever we give thought to God being in heaven—infinitely above us by the greatness of His majesty—we place ourselves in His presence with deepest sentiments of reverence. Then, seized with fear of God, we will flee pride and bow down before Him in our nothingness.

When we say the name *Father,* we remember that we owe our existence to God by means of our parents, and even our education by means of our teachers. Parents and teachers hold here the place of God, Whose living images they are. So we feel the duty to honor them or, rather, honor God in them, and to be respectful to them, taking care not to grieve them.

When we want the holy *name* of God *to be glorified,* we are far from profaning it. When we look upon the *Kingdom of God* as our heritage, *we cannot be attached to the things of this world.*

When we sincerely ask God for the same blessings for our neighbor as we want for ourselves, we will not hate, or quarrel with, or be jealous of the neighbor.

In asking God each day for our *daily bread,* we learn to abhor gluttony and sensuality, which feed on abundance.

In asking God to *forgive us as we forgive those who trespass against us,* we repress anger and thoughts of getting even; we return good for evil and we love our enemies.

In asking God not to let us fall into sin at the time of *temptation,* we show we are fleeing laziness and are seeking means of overcoming our bad habits and ensuring our salvation.

In asking God to *deliver us from evil,* we fear His justice and we are blessed, because fear of God is the beginning of wisdom. It is the fear of God that enables us to avoid sin.

FIFTEENTH ROSE
Excellence of the Hail Mary

[44] THE Angelic Salutation is so heavenly and so deep in its meaning that Blessed Alan de la Roche believed no mere creature could understand it and only our Lord Jesus Christ, born of the Virgin Mary, could explain it.

It derives its excellence mainly from three sources: from the Blessed Virgin, to whom it was addressed; from the purpose of the Incarnation of the Word, for which it was brought from heaven; and from the Archangel Gabriel, who was the first to say it.

The Angelic Salutation is the most concise summary of the whole Catholic theology concerning the Blessed Virgin. It has two parts: that of praise and that of petition. The first contains all that makes up Mary's true greatness. The second contains all we have need to ask of her and all we may expect to receive because of her goodness.

The Most Holy Trinity revealed the first part; St. Elizabeth, inspired by the Holy Spirit, added the second part; the Church, at the First Council of Ephesus, held in 431, added the conclusion to it.

This Council condemned the Nestorian heresy and defined the teaching that the Blessed Virgin is truly the Mother of God. It also said people should pray to the Virgin Mary under this glorious title in these words: "Holy Mary, Mother of God, pray for us sinners now and at the hour of our death."*

[45] The Virgin Mary was the one to whom this heavenly Salutation was presented to terminate the greatest and most important event in the history of the world: the Incarnation of the eternal Word. Through the Incarnation peace between God and us was restored and we were redeemed. The ambassador of this good news was the Archangel Gabriel, one of the leading princes of the heavenly court.

The Angelic Salutation embodies the faith and hope of the Patriarchs, the Prophets, and the Apostles. According to Blessed Alan, it gives Martyrs their steadfast courage and their fortitude,

---

* Although St. Louis attributes the words "Holy Mary . . . our death" to the Council of Ephesus (431), modern research indicates that they appeared only in the fourteenth century—inspired no doubt by that Council's identification of Mary as "Mother of God."

and it is the wisdom of the Doctors of the Church, the perseverance of Confessors, and the life of all Religious. It is also the new canticle of the law of grace, the joy of Angels and humans, and the canticle that strikes terror in the devils and puts them to shame.

Through the Angelic Salutation God became man, a Virgin became Mother of God, the souls of the righteous were delivered from Limbo, and the empty thrones in heaven were filled. In addition, sin was forgiven, grace was given us, the sick were made well, the dead were brought back to life, exiles were called home, the Blessed Trinity was appeased, and we obtained eternal life.

Finally, the Angelic Salutation is a rainbow in the sky, a sign of the mercy and grace God has given to the world.

SIXTEENTH ROSE

Beauty of the Angelic Salutation

[46] THERE is nothing so great as God in His majesty and nothing so low as human beings insofar as our sinfulness. Yet God does not disdain our acts of homage; on the contrary, He is pleased when we sing His praises.

The Salutation of the Archangel is one of the most beautiful canticles we can address to the glory of the Most High. "I will sing a new song to

You" (Psalm 144:9). The new song, which David foretold would be sung at the coming of the Messiah, was the Salutation of the Archangel.

There is an old song and a new song. The old song is the one the Israelites sang in gratitude to God for creating them and keeping them in existence; for delivering them from captivity and leading them safely through the Red Sea; for giving them manna; and for all His other blessings.

The new song is the one Christians sing in gratitude to God for the graces of the Incarnation and the Redemption. Since these wonders came about in consequence of the Angelic Salutation, we repeat this same Salutation to thank the Most Blessed Trinity for Its inestimable blessings.

We praise God the Father because He so loved the world that He gave us His only Son as our Savior. We bless the Son because He came down from heaven to us on earth and became man to redeem us. We glorify the Holy Spirit because He formed in the Blessed Virgin's womb the Body of our Lord—a most pure Body that was the victim for our sins.

It is in such a spirit of gratitude that we should say the Angelic Salutation, making acts of faith, hope, love, and thanksgiving for the gift of our salvation.

[47] Although the new song is addressed directly to the Mother of God and contains her praises, it nevertheless glorifies the Blessed Trinity. Any honor we pay to our Lady returns to God as the cause of all her perfections and virtues. God the Father is

glorified because we are honoring His most perfect creature. God the Son is glorified because we are praising His most pure Mother. God the Holy Spirit is glorified because we are in admiration of the graces with which He filled His Spouse.

The Blessed Virgin, by her beautiful canticle the *Magnificat*, returned to God the praises and blessings St. Elizabeth gave her because of her eminent dignity as Mother of God. Today, she promptly returns to God the praises and blessings we give her in the Angelic Salutation.

[48] Just as the Angelic Salutation gives glory to the Blessed Trinity, it is also the most perfect praise we can address to Mary.

St. Mechtilde was trying to think of a way by which she could show her love of the Mother of God better than she had been doing. One day, she fell into an ecstasy, and saw the Blessed Virgin with the Angelic Salutation in letters of gold upon her bosom and speaking to her: "My daughter, I want you to know that no one can honor me with a more pleasing salutation than the one that the Most Adorable Trinity presented to me and by which I was exalted to the dignity of Mother of God.

"By the word *Ave* (which is the name Eve, *Eva),* I learned that God by His omnipotence preserved me from all sin and from the miseries to which the first woman was subject.

"The name Mary, which means 'lady of light,' indicates that God has filled me with wisdom and light, like a shining star, to illumine heaven and earth.

"The words *full of grace* represent to me that the Holy Spirit has showered me with so many graces that I can share them in abundance with those who ask for them through me as Mediatrix.

"In saying *the Lord is with you,* people renew the ineffable joy that was mine when the eternal Word was made flesh in my womb.

"When people say to me *blessed are you among women,* I praise the Divine Mercy that lifted me to this exalted degree of happiness.

"At the words *blessed is the fruit of your womb, Jesus,* all heaven rejoices with me in seeing my Son Jesus adored and glorified for having redeemed humanity."

SEVENTEENTH ROSE

Wonderful Fruits of the Hail Mary

[49] AMONG the wonderful things the Holy Virgin revealed to Blessed Alan de la Roche (and we know this great devotee of Mary confirmed under oath the revelations he received), three stand out.

The first is that if people do not say the Angelic Salutation (which has saved the world) out of carelessness, or because they are lukewarm, or because they have an aversion to it, this is a sign that they will probably and shortly be condemned to eternal reprobation.

The second is that people who love this heavenly Salutation bear a very special mark of predestination.

The third is that people who have received from God the favor of loving the Blessed Virgin and serving her out of love must steadfastly continue to love and serve her. When their time on earth is up, she will have them placed by her Son in the degree of glory that befits their merits.

[50] Heretics, all of whom are children of the devil and bear the evident marks of reprobation, have a horror of the Hail Mary. They still say the Our Father but not the Hail Mary. They would rather wear a serpent around their necks than a Rosary.

Among Catholics, those who bear the mark of reprobation care very little for the Rosary (whether that of five decades or fifteen). They say it not at all or only with apathy and in haste.

Even if I lent no credence to what was revealed to Blessed Alan de la Roche, my own experience would be enough to convince me of this terrible but consoling truth. I do not know, nor do I see clearly, how a devotion that seems so small can be the infallible mark of eternal salvation, and how its absence can be the mark of reprobation. Yet nothing could be more true.

In our time, we see even people, who hold new doctrines that have been condemned by the Church, ignore the Rosary in spite of their apparent piety. They often seek to dissuade others from saying it by all kinds of pretexts intended to take it out of their minds and hearts.

They are careful not to condemn the Rosary and the Scapular, as the Calvinists are wont to do.

However, their manner of acting in order to carry out their intention is all the more dangerous because it is more cunning. We will speak of this again later on [see nos. 147-148, pp. 163-165].

[51] My Hail Mary, my Rosary, or my chaplet, is the prayer and the unerring touchstone by which I can tell people who are led by the Spirit of God from people who are deceived by the devil. I have known souls who seemed to soar heavenward like eagles by their sublime contemplation and yet were led astray by the devil. I only discovered how deceived they were when I learned they disliked the Hail Mary and the Rosary, which they rejected as being beneath them.

The Hail Mary is a heavenly dew that, falling upon the soul of a predestinate, gives it a wonderful fertility so that it can grow in all virtues. The more the soul is watered by the Hail Mary, the more the mind is enlightened and the more the soul is strengthened to overcome its spiritual enemies.

The Hail Mary is a piercing and flaming dart that, joined to the Word of God, gives the preacher the power to pierce, reach, and convert the most hardened hearts even if he does not have much natural talent for preaching. This flaming dart, the Hail Mary, is the secret the Blessed Virgin taught St. Dominic and Blessed Alan for the purpose of converting heretics and sinners.

From the example of St. Dominic and Blessed Alan came the practice of preachers to say a Hail Mary at the beginning of their sermons, as St. Antoninus tells us.

EIGHTEENTH ROSE
Blessings of the Hail Mary

[52] THIS heavenly Salutation draws down upon us the blessings of Jesus and Mary in abundance; for it is an infallible rule that Jesus and Mary reward handsomely people who glorify them. They repay us a hundredfold for the praises we give them. "I love those who love me . . . that I may enrich them and fill their treasures" (Proverbs 8:17, 21).

Jesus and Mary say: "We love those who love us; we enrich them and fill their treasuries to overflowing." "Whoever sows blessings will also reap blessings" (2 Corinthians 9:6).

If we say the Hail Mary devoutly, we love, bless, and glorify Jesus and Mary. In each Hail Mary, we bless both Jesus and Mary: "Blessed are you among women, and blessed is the fruit of your womb, Jesus."

By each Hail Mary, we render Mary the same honor God rendered her when He sent the Archangel Gabriel to greet her on His behalf.

How could anyone think that Jesus and Mary, who often do good to people who curse them, could ever curse people who bless and honor them by the Hail Mary?

St. Bernard and St. Bonaventure say that the Queen of Heaven is not less grateful and well-mannered than grateful and well-mannered people in this world. She surpasses them even in this virtue of gratitude as in all other perfections. She would never let us honor her without repaying us a hundredfold.

St. Bonaventure also says that Mary will greet us with grace if we greet her with the Hail Mary. Yet who can comprehend the graces and blessings that the greeting and tender affection of the Blessed Virgin draw down upon us?

From the moment that St. Elizabeth heard the greeting the Mother of God gave her, she was filled with the Holy Spirit and the child in her womb leapt for joy. If we make ourselves worthy of the greeting and blessings of the Blessed Virgin, we can be sure we will be filled with graces and our soul will be flooded with spiritual consolations.

NINETEENTH ROSE
Felicitous Exchange

[53] It is written: "Give and it shall be given unto you" (Luke 6:36). Let us take Blessed Alan's illustration of this: "If each day I give you one hundred and fifty diamonds, would you not forgive me, even if you were my enemy? Would you not treat me as a friend and give me all the graces you were able to give? If you want to gain the riches of grace and of glory, greet the Blessed Virgin and honor your good Mother."

"One who honors his Mother [the Blessed Virgin] is like a person who lays up a treasure" (Sirach 3:5). So every day give her at least fifty Hail

Marys. Each one is worth fifteen precious stones, which please her more than all the riches of this world combined.

What can you not expect from her generosity? She is our Mother and our friend. She is the Empress of the universe, and she loves us more than all the mothers and queens of the world have ever loved a human being. For, as St. Augustine declares, the Virgin Mary surpasses the natural love of all human beings and all the Angels.

[54] One day St. Gertrude had a vision of our Lord counting gold coins. She summoned up the courage to ask Him what He was counting. He answered: "I am counting the Hail Marys you have said; they constitute the money with which you can pay your way to heaven."

The holy and learned Jesuit, Father Suarez, regarded the Angelic Salutation so highly that he said he would gladly give up all his learning for the price of one Hail Mary devoutly said.

[55] Blessed Alan de la Roche has recourse to Mary in this way: "Let everyone who loves you, O Holy Mary, listen and rejoice. Heaven exults and the earth is in admiration whenever I say 'Hail Mary.' I hold the world in horror and have the love of God in my heart whenever I say 'Hail Mary.' My fears disappear and my passions are mortified when I say 'Hail Mary.' I grow in the devotion and am flooded with compunction when I say 'Hail Mary.' My hope is made strong and my consolation is increased when I say 'Hail Mary.'"

"The sweetness of this heavenly Salutation is so great that no words can explain it adequately. Even when its wonders have been sung, it still remains so hidden and so deep that we cannot uncover it. It is short in words but great in mysteries. It is sweeter than honey and more precious than gold. We should often meditate on it in our hearts and have it on our lips to say it devoutly again and again."

Blessed Alan says that a nun who had great devotion to the Holy Rosary appeared after her death to another nun of the same convent and said to her: "If I could go back into my body to say just one Hail Mary—even without much fervor—I would gladly again go through the sufferings I had during my last illness, in order to gain the merit of this prayer." It should be noted she had been bedridden and suffered for several years before she died.

[56] Michael de Lisle, Bishop of Salubre, who was a disciple and coworker of Blessed Alan in the reestablishment of the practice of the Holy Rosary, says that the Angelic Salutation is the remedy for all the ills that afflict us, provided we say it devoutly in honor of the Blessed Virgin.

TWENTIETH ROSE

Brief Explanation of the Hail Mary

[57] Aʀᴇ you in the miserable state of sin? Then call on Mary and say to her "Ave," which means "I greet you with the most profound respect, you who

are without sin, without evil." She will deliver you from the evil of your sins.

Are you enmeshed in the darkness of ignorance or error? Come to Mary and say to her *"Hail Mary,"* which means, "Hail, you who are enlightened by the rays of the Sun of Justice." She will share her light with you.

Have you strayed from the way to heaven? Then call on Mary. Her name means "Star of the Sea, the North Star that guides our navigation in this world." She will lead you to the port of eternal salvation.

Are you in affliction? Have recourse to Mary. Her name means "Sea of Bitterness, which has been filled with bitterness in the world and now is changed into a Sea of Purest Joy in heaven." She will turn your sadness into joy and your afflictions into consolations.

Have you lost the state of grace? Honor the abundance of graces with which God has filled the Blessed Virgin and say to her: "You are *full of grace* and all the gifts of the Holy Spirit." She will share her graces with you.

Are you all alone and deprived of God's protection? Address yourself to Mary and say to her: *"The Lord is with you* more nobly and intimately than He is with all the righteous and the Saints. You are the one with Him. He is your Son. His flesh is your flesh. You are with the Lord by a perfect likeness to Him and by a mutual love; for you are His Mother." Then say to her: "The Blessed Trinity is with you; you are Its precious Temple." She will again place you under God's protection.

Have you become the object of God's malediction? Say: *"Blessed are you above all women and all nations, by your purity and fertility; you have changed God's malediction into blessing."* And she will bless you.

Do you hunger for the bread of grace and the bread of Life? Turn to her who bore the Living Bread that came down from heaven and say to her:

"Blessed is the fruit of your womb, Whom you conceived without the loss of your virginity, Whom you carried without discomfort and to Whom you gave birth without pain. Blessed be Jesus, Who has redeemed the captive world, Who has healed the ailing world, raised the dead to life, brought home the banished, restored sinners to a life of grace, and saved us from damnation."

Without doubt, your soul will be filled with the bread of grace in this life and of eternal glory in the next. Amen.

[58] Then at the end of your prayer, pray with the Church and say:

> *Holy Mary,*
> holy in body and soul,
> holy by an incomparable and eternal devotion
> to the service of God,
> holy in the capacity of Mother of God,
> Who endowed you with eminent holiness
> befitting this surpassing dignity.
>
> *Mother of God,*
> you are also our Mother,

our Advocate and Mediatrix.
You are the Treasurer of God's graces,
and you dispense them.
Obtain for us soon
the forgiveness of our sins
and reconciliation with God's Majesty.

Pray for us sinners,
you who have great compassion
for those in need.
You do not despise sinners
or turn them away.
Without them you would not be
the Mother of the Redeemer.
Pray for us *now*,
during this short life,
fragile and miserable;
now
because we have only the present moment.
Pray for us *now*
because we are being attacked day and
   night
by powerful and ruthless enemies.

Pray for us
at the hour of our death,
so dreaded and perilous,
when our strength is waning
and our mind and body are worn out
with fear and pain.
Pray for us at the hour of our death
because then the devil is at work
to bring us to everlasting perdition,
and it will be decided

whether our lot is going to be
heaven or hell forever.

Come to the aid of your children,
Mother of pity,
Advocate and Refuge of Sinners.
Drive far from us
at the hour of death
the devils, our accusers and enemies,
whose frightful appearance fills us with
  dread.
Light our path
through the valley of death.
Lead and accompany us
to the judgment seat of your Son, our Judge.
Intercede for us
and ask Him to forgive us
and place us among the number of the elect
in the realm of everlasting glory.
Amen. So be it.

[59] Who could help admiring the value of the Rosary, made up of two heavenly parts: the Lord's Prayer and the Angelic Salutation? Are there prayers more pleasing to God and the Blessed Virgin, easier, more precious, and more helpful to us? We should always have them in our heart and on our lips to honor the Blessed Trinity, Jesus Christ our Savior, and His Most Holy Mother.

At the end of each decade, it is proper to add the *Gloria Patri,* i.e., "Glory be to the Father, and to the Son, and to the Holy Spirit. As it was in the beginning, is now, and ever shall be, world without end. Amen."

THIRD DECADE

Excellence of the Holy Rosary as a Meditation on the Life and Passion of Our Lord Jesus Christ

---

TWENTY-FIRST ROSE
The Fifteen Mysteries of the Rosary

[60] A MYSTERY is a sacred thing that is difficult to understand. The works of our Lord Jesus Christ are sacred and Divine because He is both God and Man. The works of the Blessed Virgin are very holy because she is God's most perfect creature.

The works of our Lord and His Holy Mother can rightly be called Mysteries because they are filled with countless wonders, perfections, and sublime and deep truths, which the Holy Spirit makes known to humble and simple souls who honor these Mysteries.

These works of Jesus and Mary may also be called wonderful flowers whose perfume and beauty are known only by people who come near, inhale their fragrance and uncover their beauty by attentive and serious meditation.

[61] St. Dominic divided the life of Jesus Christ and the Blessed Virgin into fifteen Mysteries, which represent their virtues and their principal actions.

These are like fifteen pictures whose traits should serve as a rule and example for the conduct of our lives. They are fifteen torches to guide our steps in this world; fifteen shining mirrors to know Jesus and Mary, to know ourselves, and to light the fire of their love in our hearts; fifteen furnaces to consume us completely by their heavenly flames.

The Blessed Virgin taught St. Dominic this excellent method of praying and ordered him to preach it to reawaken the piety of Christians and to revive in their hearts a love for Jesus Christ.

She also taught it to Blessed Alan de la Roche and said to him in a vision: "When people say a hundred and fifty Angelic Salutations, that prayer is very helpful to them and is a homage that is very pleasing to me. And this recitation of the Angelic Salutation will please me even more if those who practice it will unite it with meditation on the Life, Passion, and Glory of Jesus Christ—for such meditation is the soul of this prayer."

In fact, the Rosary said without meditating on the sacred Mysteries of our redemption would almost be like a body without a soul, excellent matter without its form. It is meditation that sets the Rosary apart from other devotions.

[62] The first part of the Rosary contains five Mysteries, of which the first is the *Annunciation* of the Archangel Gabriel to the Blessed Virgin; the second, the *Visitation* of Mary to St. Elizabeth; the third, the *Nativity* of Jesus Christ; the fourth, the *Presentation* of the Child Jesus in the Temple and

the Purification of the Virgin; and the fifth, the *Finding* of Jesus in the Temple among the doctors.

These Mysteries are called *joyful* because of the joy they gave to the whole universe. The Blessed Virgin and the Angels were overwhelmed with joy at the happy moment when the Son of God was made flesh. St. Elizabeth and St. John the Baptist were filled with joy by the visit of Jesus and Mary. Heaven and earth rejoiced at the birth of the Savior. Simeon was consoled and overcome with joy when he took Jesus in his arms. The doctors were lost in admiration when they heard the answers Jesus gave.

And who can express the joy of Mary and Joseph in finding Jesus after He had been lost for three days?

[63] The second part of the Rosary is also composed of five Mysteries, which are called the *Sorrowful* Mysteries because they show us Jesus weighed down with sadness, covered with wounds and laden with insults, sufferings, and torments. The first of these Mysteries is the prayer of Jesus and His *Agony* in the Garden of Olives; the second, His *Scourging*; the third, His *Crowning* with thorns; the fourth, His *Carrying of the Cross;* the fifth, His *Crucifixion and Death* on Calvary.

[64] The third part of the Rosary contains five other Mysteries, which are called *Glorious* because in them we meditate on Jesus and Mary in their triumph and glory. The first is the *Resurrection* of Jesus Christ; the second, His *Ascension* into heaven; the third, the *Descent of the Holy Spirit* upon

the Apostles; the fourth the *Assumption* of the glorious Virgin; the fifth, her *Crowning* in heaven.

These are the fifteen fragrant flowers of the mystical Rose Tree on which pious souls rest like industrious bees to gather their nectar and produce the honey of a solid devotion.

TWENTY-SECOND ROSE

Meditation on the Mysteries Conforms Us to Christ

[65] THE main concern of a Christian should be to tend toward perfection. St. Paul tells us, "Be followers of God, as most dear children" (Ephesians 5:1). This obligation is included in the eternal decree of our predestination, as the sole means prescribed by God to attain everlasting glory.

St. Gregory of Nyssa makes the felicitous comparison that we are all painters and our souls are the blank canvas on which we should apply the brush. The colors we should use are the Christian virtues. The model we should copy is Jesus Christ, the perfect living Image of the eternal Father.

A portrait painter keeps the model in sight and glances at the model before making each stroke. Similarly, the Christian should always have in sight the Life and virtues of Jesus Christ so as to say, think, and do nothing that is not in harmony with the Model.

[66] The Blessed Virgin wanted to help us in the great task of working out our salvation. So she ordered St. Dominic to teach the faithful who say the Rosary to meditate on the sacred Mysteries of the Life of Jesus Christ. She did this not only that they might adore and glorify Him but also that they might pattern their lives and actions on His virtues.

Children copy their parents by watching them and talking to them and they learn the language of their parents by hearing them speak. An apprentice learns his trade by watching his master at work. Similarly, the faithful members of the Confraternity of the Holy Rosary can become like their *Divine Master* if they study and imitate His virtues, which are shown in the fifteen Mysteries of *His Life*. They will be helped by His grace and by the intercession of the Blessed Virgin.

[67] Moses was inspired by God to command the Hebrew people never to forget the blessings that had been showered on them. The Son of God has all the more reason to command us to engrave the Mysteries of His Life, Passion and Glory on our hearts and to have them always before our eyes. Each Mystery reminds us of His overwhelming love for us and His desire for our salvation.

Our Lord is saying to us: "O, all you that pass by, pause a while and see if there has ever been sorrow like the sorrow I have undergone for love of you" (see Lamentations 1:12). "Be mindful of My poverty and My humiliations; think of the wine mingled with gall I drank for you during My bitter Passion" (see Lamentations 3:19).

These words and many others that could be given here should be more than enough to convince us that we ought not only to say the Rosary with our lips in honor of our Lord and the Blessed Virgin but also to say it while meditating on the sacred Mysteries.

TWENTY-THIRD ROSE

The Rosary: Memorial of the Life and Death of Jesus

[68] JESUS Christ, the Divine Spouse of our souls, our very dear Friend, wants us to remember His blessings and to esteem them more highly than anything else. He experiences an accidental joy and so do the Blessed Virgin and all the Saints in heaven whenever we meditate devoutly and lovingly on the sacred Mysteries of the Rosary.

These Mysteries are the most signal effects of Jesus' love for us and the richest gifts He could give us, because it is by virtue of such gifts that the Blessed Virgin herself and all the Saints are in their glory in heaven.

One day, Blessed Angela of Foligno asked our Lord to let her know by which religious exercise she could honor Him best. He appeared to her in a vision in which he was nailed to the Cross and He said: "My Daughter, look at My wounds." She then understood that nothing pleases this most lovable Savior more than meditating on His sufferings. Next He showed her the wounds on His head and made known to her still other sufferings and said: "I have suffered all this for your salvation. What can you do to equal My love for you?"

[69] The Holy Sacrifice of the Mass gives infinite honor to the Most Blessed Trinity because the Mass represents the Passion of Jesus Christ and through it we offer the merits of His obedience, of His sufferings, and of His Blood. The whole heavenly court receives an accidental glory from the Mass.

Several Doctors, St. Thomas included, tell us that, for the same reason, the whole heavenly court rejoices in the Holy Communion of the faithful, because the Blessed Sacrament is a memorial of the Passion and Death of Jesus Christ and by this means we share in its fruits and make progress in the work of our salvation.

The Holy Rosary, said together with meditation on the sacred Mysteries, is a sacrifice of praise to God for the blessing of our Redemption. It is also a devout reminder of the Sufferings, Death, and Glory of Jesus Christ.

Hence, it is true that the Rosary gives glory and accidental joy to Jesus Christ, the Holy Virgin, and all the Blessed in heaven, since they desire nothing greater for our everlasting happiness than to see us engaged in a practice so glorious for our Savior and so salutary for ourselves.

[70] The Gospel assures us that a sinner who is converted and does penance gives joy to all the Angels. If the repentance of one sinner is enough to rejoice the Angels, what joy, what jubilation must there be for the whole heavenly court, and what glory for our Blessed Lord Himself, to see us on earth meditating devoutly and lovingly on His humiliations and torments, on His cruel and ignominious Death? Is there anything more likely to move us and bring us to sincere repentance?

A Christian who does not meditate on the Mysteries of the Rosary is very ungrateful to our Lord and has little regard for what this Divine Savior suffered to save the world. His conduct seems to say he knows little or nothing of the Life of our Lord and has never bestirred himself to find out what He did and what He went through to save us.

A Christian of this kind ought to fear that since he has not known Jesus Christ or has put Him out of his mind, he may be disowned by our Lord on Judgment Day with the words: "Amen, I say to you, I know you not" (Matthew 25:12).

Let us, then, meditate on the Life and Sufferings of our Lord by means of the Holy Rosary. Let us learn to know Him well and also to be grateful for His blessings so that on Judgment Day He will acknowledge us as His children and His friends.

TWENTY-FOURTH ROSE

Meditation on the Mysteries of the Rosary Is a Great Means of Perfection

[71] THE principal study of the Saints was the Life of Jesus Christ. They meditated on His Virtues and His Sufferings and by this means they attained Christian perfection.

St. Bernard began with this practice, and he always continued it. "At the beginning of my conversion," he says, "I made a bouquet of myrrh consisting of the sorrows of my Savior. I put this bouquet upon my heart, thinking of the stripes, the thorns, and the nails of His Passion. I applied my whole mind to meditating every day on these Mysteries."

This was also the practice of the holy Martyrs. We admire how they triumphed over the most cruel torments. St. Bernard says that the wonderful constancy of the Martyrs could only have come from the wounds of Jesus Christ, on which they made their most frequent meditations. Where were the souls of these generous athletes of Christ while their blood flowed and their bodies were wracked with torments? They were hidden in the wounds of Jesus Christ—and these wounds made them invincible.

[72] The most holy Mother of the Savior spent much of her time in meditating on the Virtues and Sufferings of her Son. When she heard the Angels sing their hymn of joy at His birth and when she saw the shepherds adore Him in the stable, her soul

was filled with admiration and she meditated on all these wonders. She compared the greatness of the Word made flesh with His deep abasement. She thought of Him in His manger filled with straw and then of His throne in heaven and in the bosom of His eternal Father. She compared the might and wisdom of a God with the weakness and simplicity of a Baby.

The Blessed Virgin said one day to St. Bridget: "Whenever I meditated on the beauty, the modesty, and the wisdom of my Son, my heart overflowed with joy; and whenever I thought of His hands and feet that would be pierced with nails, I shed a torrent of tears and my heart was broken with sorrow and pain."

[73] After our Lord's Ascension, the Blessed Virgin spent the rest of her life visiting the places that had been sanctified by His presence and His Sufferings. When she was in those places, she used to meditate on His boundless love and the rigor of His Passion.

[According to tradition,] St. Mary Magdalene also used to meditate on the Virtues and Sufferings of our Lord in the last thirty years of her life, when she lived in Sainte-Baume.

St. Jerome says that this devotion was also widespread among the first Christians. They came to the Holy land from all countries of the world. They wanted to keep the love and remembrance of the Savior in their hearts, by seeing the places and things He had made holy by His birth, His work, His Sufferings, and His Death.

[74] All Christians have the same faith, worship the same God, and hope for the same happiness in heaven. They acknowledge only one Mediator, Who is Jesus Christ. They must all imitate this Divine Model—and in order to do so must meditate on the Mysteries of His Life, of His Virtues, and of His Glory.

It is a mistake to think that only priests and religious and people who have withdrawn from worldly concerns are required to meditate on the truths of our Faith and the Mysteries of the Life of Jesus. If priests and religious have an obligation to meditate on the truths of our Faith so as to live up to their vocation, the same obligation holds for the laity.

The reason for this obligation of the laity is that every day they are faced with spiritual dangers that could make them lose their souls. So they should arm themselves with frequent meditation on the Life, Virtues, and Sufferings of our Lord, which are presented in the fifteen Mysteries of the Holy Rosary.

TWENTY-FIFTH ROSE

The Riches of Sanctification Found in the Prayers and Meditations of the Rosary

[75] No one will ever be able to understand the wondrous riches of sanctification found in the prayers and Mysteries of the Holy Rosary. The meditation on the Mysteries of the Life and Death

of our Lord and Savior Jesus Christ is the source of the most wonderful fruits for people who use it.

People today are looking for things that strike and move them and leave deep impressions on the soul. Yet is there anything more moving in the history of the world than the wonderful story of our Redeemer, which is unfurled before our eyes in the fifteen scenes that recall the grand events of the Life, Death, and Glory of the Savior of the world?

As for the prayers of the Holy Rosary—the Lord's Prayer and the Angelic Salutation—they are more excellent and sublime than any others whatsoever. In them are expressed all our desires and needs.

[76] Meditation on the Mysteries and prayers of the Rosary is the easiest form of meditation, because the diversity of the Virtues of our Lord Jesus Christ and of the stages of His Life that we study refresh and strengthen the mind in a wonderful way and help prevent distraction.

Learned people find in the Mysteries of the Rosary the source of most profound doctrine, while simple people find in them the source of instruction that is easy for them to understand.

We must practice this easy form of meditation before progressing to the highest state of contemplation. Such is the thought of St. Thomas Aquinas and the advice he gives us when he says we must first practice, as it were, on a battlefield to acquire all the virtues of which we have the perfect model in the Mysteries of the Rosary.*

---

* *Summa Theol.* II, II, q. 182, art. 3.

The learned Cajetan says it is by meditating on the Mysteries of the Rosary that we acquire intimate union with God—for without this union, contemplation is an illusion that can lead souls astray.

[77] If the false Illuminists or Quietists of our day had followed this advice, they would not have undergone such falls nor caused such scandals among pious souls.

To think one can say prayers that are more sublime than the Our Father and the Hail Mary is an illusion that comes from the devil.

Indeed, these sublime prayers are the support, the strength, and the security of the soul.

I must admit, however, that it is not always necessary to say these prayers vocally. It is true that, in a sense, mental prayer is more perfect than vocal prayer. On the other hand, it is really dangerous, not to say pernicious, to give up saying the Rosary of your own accord under the pretext of seeking a more perfect union with God.

Sometimes, a soul that is proud in a subtle kind of way, and has done everything to rise to the sublime heights of the contemplation reached by the Saints, is deluded by the noonday devil. Thinking it has found a greater good, it gives up its former devotions as inferior and only fit for ordinary souls.

This kind of soul turns a deaf ear to the Salutation of an Archangel and even to the Prayer that God has composed, practiced, and commanded: "Thus shall you pray, 'Our Father . . .'" (Matthew 6:9). In this way, such a soul drifts from illusion to illusion, from precipice to precipice.

[78] Believe me, dear member of the Confraternity of the Rosary, if you wish to reach a high level of prayer without falling into traps set by the devil, so common to persons of prayer, say your Rosary every day, or at least five decades of it.*

If by the grace of God, you have reached a high level of prayer, keep up the practice of saying the Holy Rosary if you want to remain there and grow in humility. Never will anyone who says the Rosary every day become a formal heretic or be led astray by the devil. This is a statement I would subscribe to with my blood.

On the other hand, if God in His great mercy draws you to Him as powerfully as He drew some of the Saints while saying the Rosary, let Him do so and remain passive in His hands. Let Him work and pray in you and let Him say your Rosary in His way, and that will be enough for the day.

But if you are only in the state of active contemplation or the usual prayers of quietude, which is the state of placing yourself in the presence of God and loving Him, you have even less reason to give up saying the Rosary. Far from making you lose ground in mental prayer or in your spiritual growth, the Rosary will be for you a wonderful aid, a real Jacob's ladder with fifteen rungs. By each of these rungs you will go from virtue to virtue and

---

* St. Louis appends a footnote that gives the following lines of St. Catherine of Siena from her *Revelations:*"Anyone, righteous or sinner, who turns to Him with reverence and devotion will not be deceived or devoured by the infernal demon."

from light to light. Without danger of being misled, you will easily come to the fullness of life in Jesus Christ.

TWENTY-SIXTH ROSE
The Rosary: A Sublime Prayer

[79] IN ANY case, do not be like a certain devout but self-willed woman in Rome who is mentioned in the book *The Wonders of the Rosary*.* She was so devout that by her holy life she put to shame even the strictest religious in the Church.

One day, she went to St. Dominic to consult with him about her spiritual life and asked him to hear her confession. For penance he gave her one Rosary to say and counseled her to say a Rosary every day. She immediately began to make excuses: she had her own will-regulated set of devotions; each day she obtained the indulgence of the Stations at Rome, always wore sackcloth and a hair shirt, and used the discipline several times a week. She also fasted much and carried out acts of penance.

St. Dominic urged her again to take his advice and say a Rosary every day, but she would not hear of it. She left the confessional almost scandalized by the advice of this new spiritual director, who had tried so hard to get her to take on a devotion not to her liking.

---

* A book by a certain Cavanac, O.P.

Later, when she was at prayer, she fell into an ecstasy and had a vision of her soul appearing before our Lord's Judgment Seat. St. Michael put all her penances and other good works on one side of the scales and all her sins and imperfections on the other. The side of her good works was greatly outweighed by the side of her sins and imperfections.

Terrified, she cried for mercy. She implored the help of the Blessed Virgin, her gracious Advocate, who took the one Rosary she had said for her penance and dropped it on the side of her good works. This one Rosary was so heavy that it outweighed both her sins and her good works. The Blessed Virgin then reproved her for refusing to follow the advice of her servant St. Dominic and for failing to say the Rosary every day.

As soon as she came to herself, she rushed to throw herself at the feet of St. Dominic. She told him all that had happened, asked his forgiveness for her unbelief, and promised to say the Holy Rosary every day. By this means she rose to Christian perfection and then to the glory of everlasting life.

You who are people of prayer, learn from this the power, value, and importance of the devotion of the Holy Rosary when it is said together with meditation on the sacred Mysteries.

[80] Few Saints have reached the same heights of prayer as St. Mary Magdalene. She was lifted up to heaven seven times each day by Angels and had

learned at the feet of our Lord Himself and His Holy Mother.

Yet one day when she asked God to show her a sure way of advancing in love of Him and arriving at the height of perfection, He sent St. Michael the Archangel to tell her, on His behalf, that there was no other way to arrive at perfection than by meditating on our Lord's Passion. So St. Michael placed a Cross in front of her cave and told her to pray before it, contemplating the Sorrowful Mysteries, which she had seen take place with her own eyes.

The example of St. Francis de Sales, the great spiritual director of souls in his day, should impel you to join the Holy Confraternity of the Rosary. Great Saint that he was, he bound himself by oath to say the Rosary every day as long as he lived.

St. Charles Borromeo also said it every day and strongly recommended this devotion to his priests and seminarians as well as to all people.

St. Pius V, one of the greatest Popes who ever ruled the Church, said the Rosary every day. St. Thomas of Villanova, who was Archbishop of Valence, St. Ignatius, St. Francis Xavier, St. Francis Borgia, St. Teresa, and St. Philip Neri as well as many other illustrious people I have not mentioned were deeply devoted to the Rosary.

Follow their example: your spiritual directors will be pleased, and if they are made aware of the benefits you can derive from this devotion, they will be the first to urge you to adopt it.

TWENTY-SEVENTH ROSE

Benefits of the Rosary

[81] Allow me to give you even more reason for embracing this devotion, which many great souls have practiced. The Rosary said with meditation on the sacred Mysteries leads to the following marvelous results:

(1) it gradually gives us perfect knowledge of Jesus Christ;

(2) it purifies our souls from sin;

(3) it gives us victory over all our enemies;

(4) it makes it easy for us to practice virtue;

(5) it sets us on fire with love of Jesus;

(6) it enriches us with graces and merits;

(7) it supplies us with what is needed to pay all our debts to God and to our neighbor, and it obtains for us all kinds of graces from God.

[82] The knowledge of Jesus Christ is the science of Christians and the science of salvation. St. Paul says it surpasses all human sciences in value and perfection (Philippians 3:8). This is true:

(1) because of the dignity of its object, which is a God-Man, compared with Whom the whole universe is only a drop of dew or a grain of sand;

(2) because of its helpfulness to us, whereas human sciences only fill us with the wind and emptiness of pride;

(3) because of its utter necessity, for no one can be saved without having knowledge of Jesus

Christ, while those who know nothing of any of the other sciences will be saved so long as they are illuminated by the knowledge of Jesus Christ.

Blessed is the Rosary, which gives us this science and knowledge of Jesus Christ by means of our meditation on His Life, Death, Passion, and Glory.

The Queen of Sheba, admiring Solomon's wisdom, exclaimed: "Blessed are your domestics and your servants, who are always in your presence and hear your wisdom"(1 Kings 10:8). But far more blessed are the faithful who meditate attentively on the Life, Virtues, Suffering, and Glory of our Savior, because by this means they acquire the perfect knowledge in which eternal life consists (see John 17:3).

[83] The Holy Virgin revealed to Blessed Alan that no sooner had St. Dominic begun to preach the Rosary than the most hardened sinners were moved and wept bitterly over their sins. Even young children did unbelievable penances, and wherever St. Dominic preached the Holy Rosary such great fervor arose that sinners changed their lives and edified everyone by their penances and the amendment of their lives.

If your conscience is burdened with sin, take your Rosary and say part of it in honor of one or other Mystery of the Life, Passion, and Glory of Jesus Christ. You can be sure that while you are meditating on these Mysteries and honoring them, He will show His sacred wounds to His Father in heaven. He will plead for you and obtain for you contrition and forgiveness of your sins.

One day, our Lord said to Blessed Alan: "If only these poor sinners would say My Rosary often, they would share in the merits of My Passion and I would be their Advocate and appease the Divine Justice."

[84] This life is one of continual war and temptation. We are not fighting with enemies of flesh and blood but with the very powers of hell (see Ephesians 6:12). What better weapons could we take up to fight against them than the Prayer that our great captain taught us and the Angelic Salutation, which has cast out devils, destroyed sin, and renewed the world? What better weapons could we use than meditation on the Life and Passion of Jesus Christ?

As St. Peter says, we must arm ourselves with this thought so that we may defend ourselves against the very same enemies that our Lord conquered and that assail us every day (see 1 Peter 4:1).

"Ever since the devil was overwhelmed by the humility and Passion of Jesus Christ," says Cardinal Hugues, "he has been almost unable to attack a soul armed with meditation on the Mysteries of our Lord's Life. If he does attack such a soul, he will be shamefully defeated."

[85] "Put on the armor of God" (Ephesians 6:11). Arm yourselves with the arms of God, with the Holy Rosary, and you will crush the devil's head and stand firm against all his temptations. That is why

even the physical Rosary is such a terrible thing for the devil, and why Saints have used it to bind him and to chase him out of the bodies of people who were possessed, as some authentic records report.

[86] Blessed Alan says that a certain man had tried all kinds of devotions to cast out the evil spirit that possessed him, but without success. So he thought of wearing his Rosary around his neck; this he did and found considerable relief. He discovered that whenever he took it off the devil tormented him cruelly. So he resolved to wear it night and day. This drove the devil away for good, because such a terrible chain was more than he could bear.

Blessed Alan also testifies that by putting a Rosary around their necks he set free many people who were possessed.

[87] Father John Amat, of the Order of St. Dominic, was preaching Lenten sermons in the Kingdom of Aragon. One day, a young girl possessed by the devil was brought to him. After he had exorcised her several times to no avail, he put his Rosary around her neck. No sooner had he done so than the girl began to scream in frightful frenzy: "Take it off! Take it off! The beads are torturing me!" Filled with compassion for the girl, Father Amat took his Rosary off her.

The next night, when Father Amat was in bed, the same devils that had possessed the girl came to him and tried to seize him. But he had his Rosary clasped in his hand and no effort of the devils could wrench it from him. He beat them and chased them away, crying out: "Holy Mary, our Lady of the Rosary, help me!"

The next day, when Father Amat went to the church, he met the poor girl—still possessed—and one of the devils within her started to laugh and said mockingly: "Well, brother, if you had been without your Rosary, I would have taken care of you."

Father Amat then threw his Rosary around the girl's neck and said: "By the sacred names of Jesus and Mary His Holy Mother, and by the power of the Most Holy Rosary, I command you, evil spirits, to leave the body of this girl at once." Forced to obey, the devils left immediately, and the girl was set free.

These accounts show the power of the Holy Rosary to overcome all kinds of temptations from evil spirits and all kinds of sins, because these blessed beads put devils to flight.

TWENTY-EIGHTH ROSE
Salutary Effects Produced
by Meditating on the Passion

[88] St. Augustine assures us that there is no spiritual exercise more fruitful or more useful for our salvation than to think frequently about the Sufferings of our Lord.

St. Albert the Great, who taught St. Thomas Aquinas, learned in a revelation that by simply thinking of or meditating on the Passion of Jesus Christ Christians can gain more merit than if they had fasted on bread and water every Friday for a whole year, or had beaten themselves with their discipline once a week till the blood flowed, or had said the whole Book of Psalms every day.

If such is the case, then how great must be the merit we can gain from the Rosary, which commemorates the whole Life and Passion of our Lord.

One day, the Holy Virgin revealed to Blessed Alan that next to the Holy Sacrifice of the Mass, which is the most important and the living memorial of the Passion of Jesus Christ, there is no devotion more excellent and more meritorious than the Rosary, which is like a second memorial of the Life and Passion of Jesus Christ.

[89] Father Dorland says that in 1481 the Blessed Virgin appeared to Venerable Dominic, a Carthusian devoted to the Holy Rosary, who lived at Treves, and said to him: "Whenever one of the faithful who is in the state of grace says the Rosary while meditating on the Life and Passion of Jesus Christ, he obtains the full remission of all his sins."

She also said to Blessed Alan: "Although there are numerous indulgences attached to my Rosary, I will add many more to every fifty Hail Marys [each group of five decades] for people who say them in the state of grace and devoutly on their knees. And whoever perseveres in the devotion of the Holy Rosary, with its prayers and meditations, will be rewarded: I will obtain the full remission of the penalty and guilt for all his sins at the end of his life.

"Do not be unbelieving, as though what I say is impossible. It is easy for me to do it because I am the Mother of the King of heaven, and He calls me Full of Grace. Being full of grace, I am able to dispense grace freely to my dear children."

[90] St. Dominic was so convinced of the efficacy and value of the Holy Rosary that he seldom gave any other penance when he heard confessions. We have an example of this in the aforementioned account of the woman in Rome, to whom he gave only a single Rosary as her penance.

Confessors should walk in the footsteps of this great Saint by asking their penitents to say the Rosary together with meditation on the sacred Mysteries, rather than giving them other penances that are less meritorious, less pleasing to God, less likely to advance them in virtue, and less efficacious in helping them avoid falling into sin.

Moreover, by saying the Rosary people gain many indulgences that are not attached to many other devotions.

[91] Abbot Blosius says: "The Rosary, with meditation on the Life and Passion of Jesus Christ, is certainly very pleasing to our Lord and to the Blessed Virgin and very effective as a means of obtaining every grace. We can say it for ourselves as well as for other people for whom we wish to pray, and for the whole Church.

"Let us turn, then, to the devotion of the Holy Rosary in all our needs, and we shall infallibly obtain what we ask of God for our salvation."

TWENTY-NINTH ROSE
The Rosary: Savior of Souls

[92] ACCORDING to St. Denis there is nothing more divine, nothing more noble or pleasing to God than to cooperate in the work of saving souls and to frustrate the devil's plans to ruin them. The Son of God came down to earth for no other reason than to save souls.

He had overthrown Satan's empire by founding the Church, but the devil rallied his forces and wrought cruel violence on souls when the Albigensian heresy arose with the hatred, dissensions, and abominable vices that he spread throughout the world in the 11th, 12th and 13th centuries.

What remedy could quell these great disorders? How could Satan's forces be repelled? In the Confraternity of the Holy Rosary, the Blessed Virgin, Protectrix of the Church, has given us a most powerful means of appeasing her Son's anger, uprooting heresy, and reforming Christian morals. As events have shown, it has brought back charity and frequent reception of the Sacraments, as was the case in the first golden centuries of the Church, and it has reformed Christian morals.

[93] Pope Leo X says in his Bull that this Confraternity was founded in honor of God and the Blessed Virgin as a buttress to hold back the evils that were going to buffet the Church.

Pope Gregory XIII affirms that the Rosary was given us from heaven as a means of appeasing the

Divine anger and imploring the Blessed Virgin's intercession.

Pope Julius III adds that the Rosary was inspired by God so heaven might more easily be opened to us through the favors of our Lady.

Pope Paul III and St. Pius V declare that the Rosary was given to the faithful so they might more easily have spiritual consolation and peace.

In view of the noble purposes for which the Confraternity was founded, who would not want to join it?

[94] One day, Father Dominic, a Carthusian who was deeply devoted to the Holy Rosary, had a vision in which heaven was opened for him to see, and the whole heavenly court was gathered in wonderful array. He heard the court sing the Rosary in an enchanting melody. Each decade was in honor of a Mystery in the Life, Passion, or Glory of Jesus Christ and of the Blessed Virgin.

Father Dominic noticed that whenever the members of the court said the holy name of Mary, they bowed their heads, and at the sacred name of Jesus they genuflected and gave thanks to God for the great good He wrought in heaven and on earth through the Holy Rosary. He also saw the Saints present to God the Rosaries that Confraternity members say here on earth. He noticed too that the members of the court were praying for people who practice this devotion.

He also saw countless crowns of beautiful perfumed flowers held in readiness for people who say the Holy Rosary devoutly. He learned that by every

Rosary they say, they make a crown for themselves that they will be able to wear in heaven.

The vision of this holy Carthusian was much like the vision St. John the Beloved Disciple had, in which he saw a great multitude of Angels and Saints. They were praising and blessing Jesus Christ for all He had done and suffered for our salvation. Is this not what devout members of the Rosary Confraternity do?

[95] We should not think the Rosary is only for simple and unlearned people. It is also for educated men and women, and the greatest of them. When St. Dominic told Pope Innocent III that he had received a command from heaven to establish this holy Confraternity, the Pope gave it his approval, urged him to preach it, and said he wished to become a member himself. Even Cardinals fervently embraced this devotion, leading Cardinal Lopez to say: "Neither sex nor age nor any other condition has kept anyone away from the devotion of the Rosary."

Accordingly, members of the Confraternity have always come from all states of life: dukes, princes, and kings as well as prelates, Cardinals, and Sovereign Pontiffs. It would take too long to give all their names in this little book.

Dear reader, if you join the Confraternity, you will share in the devotion of your fellow members and in the graces they gain on earth and in their glory in heaven. Since you are united with them in their devotion, you will also share in their dignity.

THIRTIETH ROSE
Privileges of the Confraternity
of the Rosary*

[96] If privileges, graces, and indulgences make a confraternity recommendable, then the Confraternity of the Rosary is most recommended by the Church. It is most favored and most enriched with indulgences. In addition, there have scarcely been any Popes since its institution that have not opened the treasures of the Church to favor it.

Since example is more persuasive than words and even favors, Sovereign Pontiffs have found that the best way to show their high regard for the Confraternity was to join it themselves.

Here is a summary of the indulgences that the Pontiffs have granted the Confraternity of the Holy Rosary.* Our Holy Father, Innocent XI, confirmed them again on July 31, 1679, and on September 25 of the same year permitted the Archbishop of Paris to publish them:

(1) Members may gain a plenary indulgence on the day of joining the Confraternity.

(2) A plenary indulgence at the hour of death.

(3) For each Rosary of Five Mysteries said: ten years and ten quarantines.

(4) Each time members say the holy names of Jesus and Mary devoutly: seven days' indulgences.

---

* This catalogue of indulgences has long since been modified. See p. 239 for Rosary indulgences that exist in our day.

(5) Seven years and seven quarantines may be gained by those who devoutly take part in or attend the Holy Rosary Procession.

(6) Members who have gone to Confession and are truly sorry for their sins may gain a plenary indulgence on certain days by visiting the Holy Rosary Chapel in the church where the Confraternity is established. This plenary indulgence can be gained on the first Sunday of every month and on the feasts of our Lord and the Blessed Virgin.

(7) For taking part in the *Salve Regina* Procession, one hundred days' indulgence.

(8) Those who openly wear the Holy Rosary to show devotion and to set a good example may gain one hundred days' indulgence.

(9) Sick members who are not able to go to church may gain a plenary indulgence by going to Confession and receiving Holy Communion and by saying on that day the complete Rosary or at least five decades.

(10) Sovereign Pontiffs have shown their generosity toward members of the Confraternity by allowing them to gain the indulgences attached to the Stations of Rome by visiting five altars in the church where the Rosary Confraternity is established, and by saying the Our Father and the Hail Mary five times before each altar for the good of the Church. If there are only one or two altars in the Confraternity church, members should say the Our Father and the Hail Mary twenty-five times before each altar.

[97] This concession was a wonderful favor granted to Confraternity members, because in the Stational Churches plenary indulgences can be gained, souls can be delivered from purgatory, and many other indulgences can be gained by members with little effort and no expense and without leaving their own country. Even if the Confraternity is not established in the place where the members live, they can gain the same indulgences by visiting five altars in any church. This favor was granted by Pope Leo X.

The Sacred Congregation of Indulgences drew up a list of certain days on which those outside the city of Rome could gain the indulgences of the Stations of Rome. The Holy Father approved this list on March 7, 1678, and commanded that it be strictly observed. These indulgences can be gained on the following days:

All Sundays of Advent; each of the three Ember Days; also Christmas Eve, at Midnight Mass, at the Mass at Dawn, and at the Mass of the Day; the feast of St. Stephen; the feast of St. John the Evangelist; the feast of the Holy Innocents; the Circumcision and the Epiphany; the Sundays of Septuagesima, Sexagesima, Quinquagesima, and on every day from Ash Wednesday to Low Sunday inclusive; each of the three Rogation Days; Ascension Day; the Vigil of Pentecost and every day during its octave; and on each of the three September Ember Days.

Dear Confraternity members, there are many other indulgences you can gain. If you want to know about them, look up the complete list of indulgences that have been granted to members of the Rosary Confraternity. You will see the names of the Popes who granted the indulgences, the years in which they granted them, and many other particulars too numerous to be included in this summary.

FOURTH DECADE

Excellence of the Holy Rosary
as Seen in the Wonders That God
Has Worked through It

THIRTY-FIRST ROSE
Blanche of Castile and Alphonsus VIII

[98] IN A visit to Blanche of Castile, Queen of France, who was deeply grieved because twelve years after her marriage she was still childless, St. Dominic advised her to say the Rosary every day to ask God for the grace of motherhood. She faithfully carried out his advice, and in 1213, she gave birth to her eldest child, Philip.

However, the child died in infancy, and the pious queen sought the Blessed Virgin's help more than ever before. She had a large number of Rosaries given out to all members of the court and also to people in several cities of the Kingdom, asking them to join her in entreating God for the favor she desired. Thus, in 1215, St. Louis was born, the prince who was to become the glory of France and the model of all Christian kings.

[99] Alphonsus VIII, King of Aragon and Castile, had been living a sinful life and therefore had been punished by God in several ways, one of

these being that he was forced to take refuge from battle in a city belonging to one of his allies.

St. Dominic happened to be in this city on Christmas Day and preached on the Rosary as he always did, pointing out how great are the graces we can obtain through the Rosary. He mentioned, among other things, that people who said the Rosary devoutly would vanquish their enemies and would regain all they had lost.

The King was struck by these words and sent for St. Dominic to ask if what he had said about the Rosary was true. The Saint replied that it was certainly true and assured him that if he would practice this devotion and join the Confraternity, he would see for himself. The King resolved to say the Rosary every day and persevered for a year in doing so.

On the next Christmas, the Blessed Virgin appeared to the King after he had finished the Rosary and said: "Alphonsus, you have served me for a year by saying my Rosary devoutly every day, so I have come to reward you. I have obtained from my Son the forgiveness of your sins. And I am giving you this Rosary. Wear it, and I promise you that none of your enemies will be able to harm you again."

Our Lady vanished, leaving the King overjoyed and encouraged. He went in search of the Queen to tell her about the Blessed Virgin's gift and the promise that went with it. He held the Rosary to her eyes, and she recovered the sight that she had lost.

Shortly afterward, the King rallied some troops and with the help of his allies boldly attacked his enemies. He defeated them, forcing them to surrender the territory they had taken from him and to make amends for their other offenses against him. Indeed, he became so successful in war that soldiers came from all over to fight under his standard because it seemed that whenever he went to battle victory was sure to follow.

This is not surprising because he never went to battle without first saying his Rosary devoutly on his knees. He saw to it that all the members of his court joined the Confraternity of the Holy Rosary and he urged his officers and servants to be devoted to it.

The Queen also joined the Confraternity and started saying the Rosary too, and she and her husband persevered in the Blessed Virgin's service and lived very holy lives.

THIRTY-SECOND ROSE
Don Perez

[100] ST. DOMINIC had a cousin named Don Perez or Pedro who was living a sinful life. When Don Perez heard that his cousin was preaching on the wonders of the Rosary and that some people had been converted and amended their lives by means of the Rosary, he said:

"I had lost all hope of being saved, but now I am beginning to be encouraged again. I must hear this man of God."

So he went to hear St. Dominic preach. When the Saint caught sight of him, he preached against sin more zealously than ever before. From the bottom of his heart he begged God to open his cousin's eyes and let him see the miserable state of his soul.

Don Perez was at first somewhat alarmed, but not enough to resolve to change his ways. However, he came again to hear St. Dominic preach, and the Saint realized that a heart as hard as his cousin's could only be moved by something out of the ordinary. He cried out: "O Lord Jesus, grant that all who are gathered here may actually see the state of the man who had just come into Your house."

Then everybody suddenly saw that Don Perez was completely encircled by a horde of devils in the form of hideous beasts who were holding him bound by iron chains. People began to flee hither and yon in mortal terror, and Don Perez himself was even more horrified than they when he saw everyone running from him.

St. Dominic brought them all to a halt and said to his cousin: "Unhappy man that you are, acknowledge the miserable state you are in and prostrate yourself at the Blessed Virgin's feet. Take this Rosary, say it with devotion and with true sorrow for all your sins, and resolve to amend your life."

So Don Perez knelt down and said the Rosary. He then felt the need to make his Confession and did so with profound contrition. St. Dominic ordered him to say the Rosary every day. Don Perez not only promised to do so but also entered his name on the Rosary Confraternity list in his own hand.

When he left the church his face, which had a bit earlier horrified everyone, now had a glow like that of an Angel. Thereafter he persevered in devotion to the Holy Rosary, led a good life, and died a happy death.

THIRTY-THIRD ROSE
A Possessed Albigensian

[101] W HEN St. Dominic was preaching the Rosary near Carcassone, an Albigensian possessed by devils was brought to him. St. Dominic exorcised the man in the presence of a large crowd of people; it seems that over twelve thousand had come to hear him preach. The devils who possessed this wretched man were forced to answer St. Dominic's questions in spite of themselves.

They said the following:

(1) There were fifteen thousand of them in the body of this possessed man, because he had attacked the fifteen Mysteries of the Rosary.

(2) By preaching the Rosary St. Dominic terrorized the depths of hell, and he was the man they hated most in all the world because of the souls he snatched from them through devotion to the Rosary.

(3) They also revealed several other particulars.

St. Dominic placed his Rosary around the Albigensian's neck and asked the devils to tell him who, of all the Saints in heaven, was the one they feared most and therefore should be most loved and honored by us on earth.

Upon this question, they let out such terror-stricken cries that most of the people fell to the ground, gripped by fear. Then, to avoid answering, the devils began to weep and wail in such a pitiful and moving manner that many of those present were overcome with a natural pity.

The devils spoke through the mouth of the Albigensian, pleading in a heart-rending voice: "Dominic, Dominic, have pity on us; we promise that we will never hurt you. You have always had compassion for sinners and people in distress. Have pity on us, for we are in great distress. Oh, we are suffering so much; why do you take pleasure in increasing our pains? Be satisfied with the pains we are enduring. Mercy, mercy, mercy."

[102] St. Dominic was not moved by the whining words of these wretched spirits and told them he would not stop tormenting them until they had answered his question. They said they would whisper the answer in his ear so that St. Dominic alone

could hear it but no one else. The Saint insisted that they answer clearly and audibly.

Then the devils fell silent and would not say another word, disregarding St. Dominic's orders. So he knelt down and prayed to the Blessed Virgin: "O all-powerful and wonderful Virgin Mary, I implore you by the power of the Holy Rosary, command these enemies of the human race to answer my question."

As soon as he said this prayer, a glowing flame leaped out of the ears, nostrils, and mouth of the Albigensian. Everyone shook with fear, but the fire did not hurt anyone. Then the devils cried:

"Dominic, we beseech you by the Passion of Jesus Christ and by the merits of His Holy Mother and all the Saints, allow us to leave the body of this man without speaking further; for the Angels will answer your question whenever you wish. After all, why should you want to believe us? Are we not all liars? Please don't torment us any more; have pity on us."

"Woe unto you, wretched spirits, who do not deserve to be heard," St. Dominic replied, and kneeling down he prayed to the Blessed Virgin:

"O most worthy Mother of Wisdom, I am praying for the people gathered here who have already learned to say the Angelic Salutation with meditation. I beg of you, force your enemies to proclaim in public the whole truth about the Rosary."

St. Dominic had hardly finished his prayer when he saw nearby the Blessed Virgin, surrounded by a multitude of Angels. She struck the possessed man with a golden rod held in her hand and said: "Answer my servant Dominic as he has asked." (Remember, the people neither saw nor heard our Lady—only St. Dominic did.)

[103] Then the devils started screaming:

[104] "O you who are our enemy, our shame, and our ruin, why have you come from heaven just to torture us?

"O Advocate of sinners, you who snatch them from the jaws of hell, you who are the surest way to paradise, why must we, in spite of ourselves, tell the whole truth and confess before everyone who it is that is the cause of our shame and our ruin? Woe unto us, princes of darkness.

"Then listen well, you Christians. This Mother of Christ is all-powerful and she can save her servants from falling into hell. It is she who, like a sun, destroys the darkness of our intrigues and craftiness. It is she who foils our hidden plots, frustrates our snares, and renders our temptations futile and ineffective.

"We are forced to confess that not one soul that has persevered in her service has ever been damned with us. Just one sigh that she offers to the Blessed Trinity is worth more than all the prayers, vows, and aspirations of all the Saints.

"We fear her more than all the other Saints together and we have no success against her faithful servants. In fact, many Christians who call upon her when they are at the hour of death and who really deserve to be damned according to our ordinary standards are saved by her intercession.

"Oh, if only Marietta (thus in their fury they called her) had not opposed our designs and our efforts, we would have long ago conquered the Church and destroyed it, and we would have seen to it that all the Orders in the Church fell into error and infidelity!

"Now that we are constrained by force to speak, we must also tell you this: no one who perseveres in saying the Rosary will be damned. She obtains for her servants the grace of true contrition, which leads them to confess their sins and receive God's mercy and forgiveness."

Then St. Dominic had all the people say the Rosary slowly and devoutly, and a wonderful thing happened. At each Hail Mary that he and the people said together, a large group of devils came forth from the possessed man's body in the form of burning coals.

When the devils had all been expelled and the heretic was entirely free of them, the Blessed Virgin (who was still invisible) gave her blessing to all the people gathered there, and they were filled with joy.

This miracle led to the conversion of a large number of heretics who then joined the Confraternity of the Most Holy Rosary.

THIRTY-FOURTH ROSE
Simon de Montfort, Alan de l'Anvallay,
and Othère

[105] UNDER the protection of our Lady of the Rosary, Simon, Count of Montfort [1160-1218], won phenomenal victories over the Albigensians. These victories are so famous that the world has never seen anything like them.

On one occasion, he defeated ten thousand heretics with a force of five hundred men, and on another occasion he overcame three thousand men with only thirty men.

On still another occasion, with eight hundred horsemen and one thousand infantrymen he completely routed the army of the King of Aragon, which was made up of a hundred thousand men. Simon suffered the loss of only one horseman and eight soldiers.

[106] From what great perils, the Blessed Virgin also protected Alan de l'Anvallay, a Breton Knight, who was fighting for the Faith against the Albigensians. One day, when he found himself surrounded by his enemies, the Blessed Virgin let fall one hundred and fifty rocks upon his enemies and delivered him from their hands.

On another day when l'Anvallay's ship foundered and was about to sink, this good Mother caused one hundred and fifty small hills to appear miraculously above the water and by means of them he reached Brittany in safety.

L'Anvallay built a monastery at Dinan for the new Order of St. Dominic in thanksgiving to the Blessed Virgin for all the miracles she had worked on his behalf in response to his daily Rosary. He became a religious himself and died a holy death at Orléans.

[107] Othère also was a Breton soldier, from Vancouleurs, and he often routed whole companies of heretics or robbers simply by wearing his Rosary on his arm or carrying it on the hilt of his sword.

Once when Othère had defeated his enemies, they acknowledged that they had seen his sword gleam and that another time they had noticed a shield on his arm with the images of our Lord, the Blessed Virgin, and the Saints on it. This shield rendered him invisible and gave him great power in combat.

Another time, Othère defeated twenty thousand heretics with only ten companies and without the loss of a single man.

This so impressed the general of the heretical army that he sought out Othère afterward, abjured his heresy, and declared that he had seen him surrounded by flaming swords during the battle.

THIRTY-FIFTH ROSE

Cardinal Pierre

[108] BLESSED Alan says that a Cardinal named Pierre, whose titular church was St. Mary-beyond-the-Tiber, was introduced to the practice of the Holy Rosary by his close friend St. Dominic and so cultivated this devotion that he became a veritable apostle of it.

Eventually, he was sent as Legate to the Holy Land to help the Crusaders who were fighting the Saracens. So thoroughly did he convince the Christian army of the power of the Rosary that all the soldiers said it in order to plead for heaven's help in a battle in which they knew they would be greatly outnumbered.

The end result was that three thousand Christians gained a victory over an enemy of one hundred thousand.

As we have seen, the devils have an overwhelming fear of the Rosary. St. Bernard says that the Angelic Salutation puts the devils to flight and causes hell to tremble.

Blessed Alan assures us that he has seen several people delivered from Satan's bondage after they had taken up the Rosary. These were people who had sold themselves in body and soul to Satan by renouncing their Baptism and Jesus Christ.

THIRTY-SIXTH ROSE
A Woman in Antwerp Delivered
from the Chains of the Devil

[109] In 1578, a woman in Antwerp had given herself to the devil, even signing the contract with her own blood. Soon thereafter she was stricken with acute remorse and had a profound desire to make amends for this evil deed. She sought out a wise and kind confessor, who advised her to go to Father Henry, director of the Confraternity of the Holy Rosary, at the Dominican Friary, to ask him to inscribe her in it and to hear her Confession.

Accordingly, she went to ask for Father Henry but instead met the devil disguised as a religious. The devil scolded her pitilessly and said she could never hope to receive God's grace again as long as she lived and there was no way she could take back what she had signed.

Although she was devastated, the woman did not lose hope of God's mercy and sought out Father Henry once more. She found the devil a second time and met with the same rebuff.

The woman came back a third time and then, by Divine Providence, she found Father Henry, the priest she had been seeking. He treated her with great kindness and urged her to throw herself upon God's mercy and make a good Confession. He then inscribed her in the Confraternity and told her to say the Rosary frequently.

One day, while Father Henry was saying Mass for her, the Blessed Virgin forced the devil to give her back the contract she had signed. In this way, she was delivered from the devil through the authority of Mary and through her devotion to the Rosary.

THIRTY-SEVENTH ROSE

A Convent Reformed through the Rosary

[110] A NOBLEMAN who had several daughters placed one of them in a convent where, unknown to him, the nuns were very proud and thought only of worldly pleasures. The nuns' confessor, on the contrary, was a man of God who had great love for the Holy Rosary.

Wishing to guide this nun to a better way of life, the confessor told her to say the Rosary every day in honor of the Blessed Virgin while meditating on the Life, Passion, and Glory of Jesus Christ.

The new religious loved this devotion and little by little was repulsed by the wayward habits of the other nuns. She began to develop a love for silence and prayer in spite of the fact that the other nuns despised and ridiculed her and called her a fanatic.

At the same time, a holy priest, who was carrying out the visitation of the convent, had a disturbing vision while he was at prayer. He seemed to see a nun in her room, at prayer in the presence of a Lady of outstanding beauty who was surrounded by Angels. The Angels held flaming spears with which they repelled a multitude of devils who were attempting to come in.

These evil spirits then fled to the other nuns' rooms under the form of vile animals in order to lead them into sin—with some of the nuns unfortunately succumbing.

By this vision, the priest came to understand the deplorable state of the convent, and thought he was about to die of sorrow. Sending for the young nun, he exhorted her to persevere.

As the priest pondered the excellence of the Rosary, he decided to reform the nuns by means of it. He bought some beautiful Rosaries and gave one to each nun, exhorting them to say the Rosary every day. He promised he would not try to force them to alter their lives if they would say the Rosary every day. Amazingly, the nuns accepted the Rosaries and promised to say them on that condition.

Little by little, the nuns gave up their worldly pursuits, applied themselves to silence and recollection, and in less than a year they all asked that the convent be reformed.

Hence, the Rosary brought about more changes in their hearts than the priest could have done by exhorting and commanding.

THIRTY-EIGHTH ROSE

A Spanish Bishop's Devotion to the Rosary

[111] A SPANISH Countess who had been instructed about the devotion of the Holy Rosary by St. Dominic said it faithfully every day and was achieving great progress in virtue. Since her only thought was how she might attain to perfection, she asked a Bishop who was a renowned preacher to suggest some practices that would help her reach her goal.

The Bishop told her that before he could make any suggestions she would have to tell him the state of her soul and also what her religious practices were. She answered that her most important religious practice was the Rosary, which she said every day while meditating on the Joyful, Sorrowful, and Glorious Mysteries, and that her soul received great spiritual help from it.

The Bishop was overjoyed to hear her explain the priceless lessons the Mysteries contain. He said, "I have been a Doctor of Theology for twenty years and have come across many excellent practices of devotion. But never have I encountered one that is more fruitful or more conformed to Christianity than the Rosary. From now on I shall follow your example and preach the Rosary."

The Bishop's preaching met with great success. In little time, his diocese changed for the better. There was a rise in conversions, restitutions, and renunciations with a marked decline in worldliness, immorality, and gambling. Peace within families, religious fervor, and Christian charity began to flourish. These changes were even more remarkable because the Bishop had previously been working hard to reform his diocese but had achieved hardly any results.

The better to promote the devotion of the Rosary, the Bishop also wore a beautiful Rosary at his side and always showed it to the people when he preached. He used to say:

"My dear people, I assure you that the Rosary of the Blessed Virgin is so excellent that although I am your Bishop and a Doctor of Theology as well as a Doctor of Canon and Civil Law, I take more pride in wearing the Rosary as the most illustrious mark of my Episcopacy and Doctorate."

THIRTY-NINTH ROSE

A Parish Renewed through the Rosary

[112] A DANISH pastor was often wont to say—for the greater glory of God and the joy of his soul— that the same improvement the Spanish Bishop noticed in his diocese had occurred in his own parish. He said:

"I had preached on the most important and fruitful aspects of Faith, with no profit at all. I saw no spiritual improvement and so I resolved to preach the Holy Rosary.

"I told the people of my parish how precious the Rosary was and I taught them how to say it. I can state that after my people practiced this devotion for six months, I saw a most visible change in them.

"Truly this God-given prayer has divine power to touch our hearts and fill them with horror of sin and love of virtue."

One day, our Lady said to Blessed Alan: "Just as God chose the Angelic Salutation to bring about the Incarnation of His Word and the Redemption of the world, so those who desire to reform the morals of people and to regenerate them in Jesus Christ must honor me and greet me with the same Salutation.

"I am the chosen way by which God came to the world, and so, next to my Son Jesus Christ, it is through me that the world must obtain grace and virtue."

[113] I, who am writing this, have learned through personal experience that the Rosary has the power to convert the most hardened hearts. I have known people upon whom the most terrifying truths preached at missions had no impression at all. Yet when, upon my recommendation, they started saying the Rosary every day they were converted and gave themselves wholeheartedly to God.

When I have gone back to visit parishes where I had conducted missions, I have seen a tremendous difference between one parish and another. In parishes where people had given up the Rosary, they had usually reverted to their sinful ways. But in parishes where people said the Rosary faithfully,

I found that they were persevering in the grace of God and growing each day in virtue.

———————

FORTIETH ROSE
Admirable Effects of the Rosary

[114]   B<small>LESSED</small> Alan de la Roche, Father John Dumont, Father Thomas, the Chronicles of St. Dominic, and other writers have often been eyewitnesses of the things whereof they speak. They have seen marvelous conversions brought about by this devotion of the Rosary. They have seen great sinners, men and women, converted after twenty, thirty, and even forty years of sin and all kinds of disorder, because they persevered in saying the Rosary.

These have been people who previously had been deaf to all pleading. Here I will not tell you about the wonderful conversions because I do not want to make this book too lengthy. I am not even going to refer to the conversions I have seen with my own eyes. There are several reasons why I would rather not talk about them.

Dear reader, if you practice this devotion and teach it to others, you will learn more by your own experience than from any spiritual book. What is

more, you will have the happiness of being rewarded by the Blessed Virgin in accordance with the
promises she made to St. Dominic, to Blessed Alan
de la Roche, and to all who practice and encourage
this devotion, which is dear to her.

For the Rosary teaches people about the virtues
of Jesus and Mary and leads them to mental prayer
and to imitation of Jesus Christ. It teaches them to
receive the Sacraments often, to strive after
Christian virtue, and to do all kinds of good works.
It also teaches them to interest themselves in the
many wonderful indulgences that can be gained
through the Rosary.

People are often not aware of the richness of the
Rosary in indulgences. The reason is that many
who preach on the Rosary hardly ever mention
indulgences and give popular sermons that excite
admiration but teach very little.

[115] I shall say no more than to assure you, in
the words of Blessed Alan de la Roche, that the
Rosary is the source and storehouse of all kinds of
blessings. Through the Holy Rosary:

(1) Sinners are forgiven.
(2) Those who thirst for perfection are re-
     freshed.
(3) Those who are fettered have their bonds
     broken.
(4) Those who weep find happiness.
(5) Those who are tempted find peace.
(6) The poor receive help.
(7) Religious are reformed.

(8) The ignorant are instructed.

(9) The living triumph over pride.

(10) The dead have their pains eased by suffrages.

One day, the Blessed Virgin said to Blessed Alan: "I want those devoted to my Rosary to have my Son's grace and blessing during their lifetime and at their death, and after their death. I want them to be freed from every type of slavery so that they will be like kings with crowns on their heads and scepters in their hands, in eternal glory. Amen."

FIFTH DECADE

The Manner of Saying the Rosary Worthily

FORTY-FIRST ROSE
Purity of Soul

[116] IT IS not the length but the fervor of a prayer that pleases God and wins His Heart. One Hail Mary said well is worth more than a hundred and fifty said badly.

Most Catholics say the Rosary, either the fifteen Mysteries or five of them or at least a few decades. Why is it, then, that so few Catholics give up their sins and advance in the spiritual life? Surely, it is because they are not saying their Rosary with fervor.

[117] Let us see how we should pray the Rosary if we want to please God and become more holy.

(1) First of all, we must be in the state of grace or at least be determined to give up mortal sin. We know this because all theology teaches us that good works and prayers are dead works if they are done in the state of mortal sin. Therefore, they can neither be pleasing to God nor help us gain eternal life. This is why Scripture says: "Praise is not seemly in the mouth of a sinner" (Sirach 15:9).

Praise of God and the Angelic Salutation and even the very Prayer of Jesus are not pleasing to God when they issue from the mouths of unrepentant sinners.

Our Lord said: "This people honors me with their lips, but their hearts are far from Me" (Mark 7:6). It is as though He was saying: "People who join My Confraternity and say their chaplet or Rosary every day, but without being sorry for their sins, offer Me lip service only and their hearts are far from Me."

(2) I have stated that to say the Rosary well we must be in the state of grace "or at least be determined to give up mortal sin."

(a) For if it were absolutely necessary to be in the state of God's grace to offer prayers pleasing to God, it would follow that those in mortal sin should never pray whereas they are the ones more in need of praying than the righteous. This is an error condemned by the Church and we can understand why: if such were the case, one could never advise sinners to pray the Rosary because it would be useless for them!

(b) If sinners join one of the Blessed Virgin's Confraternities and say the Rosary or some other prayer without the intention of giving up sin, they join the ranks of her false devotees. These impenitent devotees, hiding under her mantle, wearing the scapular, and having Rosary in hand, cry out: "Blessed Virgin, good Mother—Hail Mary!" And yet, at the same time, by their sins they are crucifying Jesus and cruelly tearing His flesh anew, and they fall from the very ranks of the Holy Virgin's Confraternities into the fires of hell.

[118] We beg everyone to say the Holy Rosary: the righteous that they may persevere and grow in

God's grace; the wicked that they may rise from their sins. But God forbid that we should ever encourage sinners to turn Mary's mantle of protection into a mantle of damnation, hiding their sins under it, and to convert the Rosary—which is a cure for all ills—into a deadly poison. There is no greater corruption than that in which the best becomes the worst.

The learned Cardinal Hugues says: "We should really be as pure as Angels to approach the Blessed Virgin and say the Angelic Salutation."

One day, our Lady appeared to an immoral man who used to say his Rosary every day. She showed him a bowl of beautiful fruit, but the bowl itself was covered with filth. The man was horrified to see this, and Mary said: "This is the way you are honoring me! You are giving me beautiful roses in a filthy bowl. You be the judge as to whether I find them pleasing!"

FORTY-SECOND ROSE
Attentive Recitation

[119] To PRAY well it is not enough to express our petitions by means of the most beautiful of all prayers, the Rosary. We must also pay attention to what we are saying, for God listens more to the voice of the heart than the voice of the mouth. To be guilty of willful distractions during prayer would show gross irreverence, which would render our Rosaries fruitless and fill us with sins.

How can we expect God to listen to us if we do not pay heed to what we are saying, and if, in the presence of His tremendous Majesty—which looks at the earth and makes it tremble—we give in to distractions just as children run after butterflies? Those who do this forfeit God's blessing and risk having it changed into a curse because they have been praying disrespectfully. "Cursed be he who does the work of the Lord deceitfully" (Jeremiah 28:10).

[120] Of course, you cannot say your Rosary without having a few involuntary distractions. Indeed, it is hard to say even one Hail Mary without your imagination taking away some of your attention (for the imagination is never still). What you can do is to say your Rosary without voluntary distractions and take every precaution to control your imagination and lessen unwanted distractions.

With this in mind, put yourself in the presence of God: imagine that God and His Blessed Mother are watching you, and your Guardian Angel, standing at your right hand, is taking your Hail Marys, if they are said attentively, and using them like roses to make crowns for Jesus and Mary.

At the same time, remember that at your left hand lurks the devil ready to lay hold of your Hail Marys that come his way and to write down in his book of death if they are not said attentively, devoutly, and reverently.

Above all, remember to offer up each decade in honor of one of the Mysteries and while saying it try to form a picture in your mind of Jesus and Mary in relation to this Mystery.

[121] The life of Blessed Hermann (a Premonstratensian Father) tells us that at one time he used to say the Rosary attentively and devoutly while meditating on the Mysteries. The Blessed Virgin then used to appear to him in brilliant light and resplendent beauty and majesty.

But with the passage of time, Hermann's fervor waned and he fell into the habit of saying his Rosary hurriedly and inattentively.

Then one day the Blessed Virgin appeared to him again, but she was now far from beautiful. Her face was wrinkled, sad, and haggard. Blessed Hermann was astonished at the change in her, but our Lady explained:

"Hermann, I am appearing to you in this fashion to show you how you now regard me in your soul— as a woman to be despised and of no importance. Why do you no longer greet me with respect and attention when meditating on my Mysteries and praising my privileges?"

FORTY-THIRD ROSE
Diligently Overcoming Distractions

[122] No other prayer gives Jesus and Mary more glory and is more meritorious for the soul than the Rosary that is said properly. But it is also the hardest prayer to say properly and takes great effort to

persevere in, especially because of the distractions that flow almost naturally from the frequent repetition of the same prayer.

When we say the Little Office of the Blessed Virgin, or the Seven Penitential Psalms, or any other prayers than the Rosary, the diversity of words and variety of expressions with which these prayers are composed prevent our imagination from wandering and refresh the mind, making it easier for us to say them attentively.

On the other hand, in saying the Rosary, which consists in the constant repetition of the Our Father and Hail Mary in the exact same form, it is difficult for us not to give in to boredom or even to sleep. Then this leads us to turn to other prayers that are more refreshing and less tedious. Hence, we need much greater devotion to persevere in saying the Rosary than in saying any other prayer, be it even the Psalter of David.

[123] What makes our task even harder is our imagination, which does not stand still even for one moment, and the malice of the devil who is indefatigable in distracting us and preventing us from praying. To what lengths does the evil one go against us when he sees us intent on saying the Rosary so as to ward off his snares!

He increases our natural languor and negligence. Before we even begin our prayer, he intensifies our boredom, distractions, and weariness. During the course of our prayer, he assails us at every turn. And when we finish praying with much effort and many distractions, he whispers to us:

"You have said nothing that has any worth; your Rosary has no value. You would have been better off to work and attend to your affairs. Don't you realize that you are wasting your time mumbling so many vocal prayers inattentively, whereas a half hour's meditation or spiritual reading would be much better for you? Tomorrow, when you are not feeling so sleepy, you will pray with more attention. So leave the rest of your Rosary for tomorrow."

By such ruses, the devil succeeds in getting us to give up the Rosary in whole or in part or at least to postpone its recitation.

[124] Dear friend of the Rosary Confraternity, do not listen to the devil and do not lose heart if during the Rosary your imagination was filled with distractions and capricious thoughts that you tried your best to cast out as soon as you became aware of them.

Remember that your Rosary is the best when it is meritorious for you; and it is more meritorious when it is difficult than when it is easy; and it is more difficult when it is distasteful to the soul and more disturbed by the little flies and ants running about in your imagination and scarcely allowing you time to appreciate the beauty of what you are saying and to take your rest in peace.

[125] Even if you have to overcome distractions all through your Rosary, be sure to fight courageously, arms in hand. Do not stop saying your Rosary even if it is hard to say and you feel no sensible consolation. It will be a terrible battle but one that profits the faithful soul. If you put down your

weapons and give up the Rosary, you admit defeat. Then, having won, the devil will leave you alone.

But on the Day of Judgment the devil will taunt you because of your infidelity and lack of courage. "Whoever is faithful in little things is also faithful in those that are greater"(Luke 16:10).

Whoever fights even the smallest distractions faithfully when saying the shortest prayer will also be faithful in fending off greater distractions. We are certain of this because the Holy Spirit has told it to us.

So all of you good and faithful servants of Jesus and His Holy Mother, who have made up your minds to say the Rosary every day, take courage! Do not let the host of flies (which I call the distractions that make war on you during prayer) make you abandon the company of Jesus and Mary, in whose holy presence you always are when you are saying the Rosary. I will now offer you some ways for lessening distractions.

FORTY-FOURTH ROSE
How To Say the Rosary

[126] F$_{\text{IRST}}$ ask the Holy Spirit to help you say the Rosary attentively. Then for a moment put yourself in the presence of God and offer up the decades in the way you will be shown later.*

Before beginning a decade, pause for a moment or two, depending on how much time is available,

---

* See pp. 171ff.

and meditate on the Mystery you are about to celebrate in that decade. Then always ask, through this Mystery and through the intercession of the Blessed Virgin, for one of the virtues that stand out most in this Mystery or one for which you have the most need.

Be sure to guard against the two common faults that most people who say the Rosary commit. The first is failing to formulate any intention before beginning. If you ask them why they are saying the Rosary, they do not know what to answer. That is why, when saying the Rosary, we should have in view some graces to ask for, some virtue to imitate, or some sin to overcome.

The second fault people ordinarily commit when saying the Rosary is to have no other intention than getting it over quickly. This comes from looking at the Rosary as a burdensome thing that weighs on our conscience when we have not said it, especially when we have made it a rule of conscience or have received it almost unwillingly as a penance.

[127] It is sad to see how most people recite the Rosary. They say it with incredible speed, even mangling the words. We would be ashamed to pay this type of compliment to even the least important of persons—and yet we think that Jesus and Mary are honored by it!

Why should we be surprised, then, if the most sacred prayers of the Christian religion remain almost without fruit and if after reciting thousands and even tens of thousands of Rosaries people are no holier than before.

Dear Confraternity members, eliminate the haste that comes almost naturally when saying your Rosary. Pause several times as you say the Our Father and Hail Mary. I have placed a cross at each pause, as shown below.

Our Father, Who art in heaven, ✠
hallowed be Thy name; ✠
Thy kingdom come; ✠
Thy will be done ✠
on earth as it is in heaven. ✠
Give us this day ✠
our daily bread; ✠
and forgive us our trespasses ✠
as we forgive those who trespass against us; ✠
and lead us not into temptation, ✠
but deliver us from evil. Amen.

Hail Mary, full of grace, ✠
the Lord is with you! ✠
Blessed are you among women, ✠
and blessed is the fruit of your womb, Jesus. ✠
Holy Mary, Mother of God, ✠
pray for us sinners, now ✠
and at the hour of our death. Amen. ✠

On account of your bad habit of saying prayers hurriedly, at first you may find it difficult to make these pauses, but a decade recited recollectedly in this way is more meritorious for you than thousands of Rosaries said in a rush, without reflection or pauses.

[128] Blessed Alan de la Roche and other writers (including St. Robert Bellarmine) tell the story

of a good confessor who advised three of his penitents, who were sisters, to say the Rosary every day for a whole year. This they did so they could make beautiful robes of glory for the Blessed Virgin out of their Rosaries. It was a secret the priest said he had received from heaven.

The three sisters said the Rosary faithfully for a year. On the Feast of the Purification, our Lady appeared to them at night when they had gone to bed. St. Catherine and St. Agnes were with her. She was wearing a beautiful robe bathed in light, and all over it "Hail Mary, full of grace" was emblazoned in letters of gold.

The Queen of heaven came to the eldest sister and said: "I greet you, my daughter, who have greeted me so often and so beautifully. I have come to thank you for the beautiful robes you have made for me."

The two virgin Saints who were with the Blessed Virgin thanked her too, and then all three of them disappeared.

An hour later, the Blessed Virgin returned, accompanied by the same two Saints. This time she was wearing a green robe that had no gold lettering and was not bathed in light. Going up to the second sister, our Lady thanked her for the robe she had made for her by saying her Rosary. Since this sister had seen our Lady appear to the eldest more magnificently dressed, she asked the reason for the change. Our Lady answered: "Your sister made me more beautiful robes because she has been saying her Rosary better than you."

About an hour later, the Blessed Virgin appeared to the youngest sister wearing torn and dirty rags. She said, "My daughter, I want to thank you for these clothes that you have made for me." The young girl was covered with shame and she called out: "O my Lady, how could I have dressed you so badly! I beg you to forgive me. Please grant me a little more time to make you a beautiful robe by saying my Rosary better."

The Blessed Virgin and the two Saints disappeared, and the girl was heartbroken. She told her confessor everything that had happened. He urged the sisters to say the Rosary for another year and to say it more devoutly than ever before.

At the end of the second year on the same day of the Purification, the Blessed Virgin, clothed in a truly magnificent robe and accompanied by St. Catherine and St. Agnes who were wearing crowns, appeared to the three sisters again in the evening. She said to them: "My daughters, you are assured of the kingdom of heaven; and you will have the great joy of going there tomorrow." The three of them cried out: "Our hearts are ready, dearest Queen, our hearts are ready." Then the vision ended.

That same night the three sisters became ill and sent for their confessor, who brought them the Last Sacraments. They thanked him for the holy practice of saying the Rosary that he had taught them. After Compline, the Blessed Virgin appeared with a multitude of virgins and had the three sisters dressed in white gowns. While Angels were singing "Come, spouses of Jesus Christ, receive the crowns that have been prepared for you for all eternity," they departed from this life.

We can learn some important truths from this story:

(1) How important it is to have a good director who will counsel holy practices of piety, especially the practice of saying the Rosary.

(2) How important it is to say the Rosary with attention and devotion.

(3) How kind and merciful the Blessed Virgin is to people who are sorry for the past and are firmly resolved to do better in the future.

(4) How generous she is in rewarding us in life, in death, and in eternity, for the little services we render faithfully to her.

FORTY-FIFTH ROSE

Saying the Rosary with Reverence

[129] I SHOULD like to add that the Rosary ought to be said with reverence, i.e., as far as possible we should be kneeling, with our hands joined and clasping the beads. However, the sick can say it in bed, people on the road can say it while walking, and those who are unable to kneel can say it while sitting or standing.

The Rosary can also be said while working, when we have things that cannot be set aside. Manual work is not always incompatible with vocal prayer.

Since the soul has its limitation and we can do only so much, when we are concentrating on manual work we cannot give our undivided attention to things of the spirit, such as prayer. Yet in time of need, this kind of prayer is not without merit in the eyes of the Blessed Virgin, who rewards our goodwill more than our external actions.

[130] I advise you to divide your Rosary into three parts and to say the five decades of each part at different times of the day. It is better to divide it than to say all fifteen decades at once.

If you cannot find the time to say a third part of the Rosary at one time, say it gradually, a decade here and a decade there. I assure you that in spite of your work you will have said the whole Rosary before going to bed.

We would do well to follow the example of the faithfulness of St. Francis de Sales. Once, exhausted by his visits of the day, he remembered toward midnight that he had left a few decades of his Rosary unsaid. He refused to go to bed until he had finished them on his knees despite all the efforts of his secretary, who saw he was tired and begged him to leave the rest of the decades for the morrow.

Let me also remind you to imitate the faithfulness, reverence, and devotion of the holy friar who is mentioned in the Chronicles of St. Francis of Assisi and who always said his Rosary very devoutly and reverently before dinner. (I have told this story earlier in the book—see "Seventh Rose: Crown of Roses," p. 40.)

FORTY-SIXTH ROSE
Saying the Rosary in Common
and in Two Choirs

[131] THERE are several ways of saying the Holy Rosary. The one that gives God the highest glory, does the most good for the soul, and strikes the greatest fear in the devil is the way of saying or chanting it publicly in two choirs.

God is pleased to have people gather for prayer. The Angels and the Blessed in heaven join together to praise Him unceasingly. The righteous on earth in several communities join in common prayer night and day. Our Lord expressly recommended common prayer to His Apostles and disciples and promised that whenever two or three were gathered in His name He would be there in the midst of them (Matthew 18:20).

What a wonderful thing to have Jesus in our midst. The only thing we have to do to get Him to come is to say the Rosary in common. This is why the early Christians often gathered to pray in spite of the Roman Emperors' persecutions and the fact that gatherings were forbidden. They preferred to expose themselves to the danger of death rather than to miss their gatherings and fail to enjoy the company of Jesus.

[132] This public way of prayer is the greatest good for the soul because of the following reasons:

(1) Ordinarily our mind is more alert during public prayer than it is when we are praying alone.

(2) When we pray in common, the prayers of the individuals belong to the whole assembly and make but one great prayer. Hence, if some are not praying well, others in the same gathering who are praying better may make up for their deficiency. In this way, the strong uphold the weak, the fervent inspire the lukewarm, the wealthy enrich the poor, and the bad are counted as good.

How can a measure of cockle be sold? It is enough to mix it up with four or five barrels of good wheat, and everything will get sold!

(3) One who says the Rosary alone only gains the merit of one Rosary, but if he says it together with thirty other people he gains the merit of thirty Rosaries. This is the law of public prayer. How profitable, how advantageous!

(4) Urban VIII was pleased to see that devotion to the Holy Rosary had spread to Rome and that it was being said in two groups or choirs, particularly at the convent of *Santa Maria Sopra Minerva*. He attached one hundred days' extra indulgence, toties quoties, whenever the Rosary was said in two choirs. This is set forth in his brief *Ad perpetuam rei memoriam* written in 1626. So every time we say the Rosary in two groups, we gain one hundred days' extra indulgence.

(5) Public prayer is far more powerful than private prayer to appease God's anger and call down His mercy. The Church, guided by the Holy Spirit, has always advocated public prayer in time of public tragedy and the suffering that goes with it.

In a Bull about the Rosary, Pope Gregory XIII declares that we must believe on pious faith that the public prayers and processions of the members of the Confraternity of the Rosary contributed much to the great victory carried off by Christians in the Gulf of Lepanto against the Turkish armada on the First Sunday of October in 1571.

[133] When King Louis the Just of blessed memory, was besieging La Rochelle, where the revolutionary heretics had their stronghold, he wrote to his mother to ask her to order public prayers so that a victory could be obtained. The Queen-Mother decided to have the Rosary said publicly in Paris in the Dominican Church of Faubourg, Saint Honore. This was done by the Archbishop of Paris. The Rosary was begun on May 20, 1628.

Both the Queen-Mother and the reigning Queen attended the recitation of the Rosary together with the Duke of Orléans, Cardinal de la Rochefoucault, and Cardinal de Bérulle, other prelates, members of the court, and an imposing crowd of people.

The Archbishop read the meditations on the Mysteries aloud and then began the Our Father and Hail Marys of each decade. The congregation, made up of religious and laypeople answered him. At the end of the Rosary, a statue of the Blessed

Virgin was solemnly carried in procession while the Litany of the Blessed Virgin was sung.

The devotion was kept up with admirable fervor every Saturday and resulted in a manifest blessing from heaven. For on All Saints' Day of the same year (1628) the King defeated the English on the Island of Ré and made his triumphant entrance to La Rochelle. This clearly shows the great power of public prayer.

[134] When the Rosary is said in common, it is far more frightening to the devil than one said privately, because it constitutes an army that is attacking him. He can easily overcome the prayer of an individual, but if this prayer is joined to that of other Christians, the devil finds it much more difficult to overcome. It is easy to break a single stick, but if you join it to others to make a bundle, it cannot be broken.

"In union there is strength." Soldiers join in an army to defeat their enemies. Wicked people often get together for debauchery and dancing. Evil spirits join together to make us lose our souls. Why, then, should not Christians join together to enjoy the presence of Jesus, to appease God's anger, to draw His grace and mercy upon them, and to better overcome the devil and his minions more vigorously?

Dear members of the Confraternity, whether you live in town or in the country, near the parish church or near a chapel, go there together (with the parish priest's permission) with all the people who want to say the Rosary in two choirs. If a church or chapel is not available, say the Rosary together in your own or a neighbor's house.

[135] This is a holy practice that God, in His mercy, has established in places where I have preached missions, to safeguard and increase their fruits and to impede sin.

Before the Rosary took root in these small towns and villages, one saw only dances, intemperance, dissoluteness, immodesty, swearing, quarrels, and feuds. One heard nothing but evil songs and double-meaning words.

Now nothing is heard but the singing of hymns and the chanting of the Our Father and Hail Mary. Nothing is seen but holy gatherings consisting of twenty, thirty, or a hundred people who, at a regular time, sing God's praises, in the manner of religious. There are even places where the Rosary is said in common, five Mysteries at a time, at three different times of the day. What a blessing from heaven!

There are wicked people everywhere, so you can be sure that they will also be where you live. There will be some who avoid coming to church for the Rosary. They may even poke fun at it and do everything in their power—by their words and their actions—to stop you from persevering in this holy practice.

However, do not give up and do not be surprised by their way of acting. Since these wretched souls will have to be separated from God and heaven for all eternity, they also have to be separated already here on earth from the company of Christ our Lord and His servants.

FORTY-SEVENTH ROSE

Saying the Rosary Every Day with Faith, Humility, and Confidence and the Necessity of Prayer

[136] PEOPLE of God, predestinate souls, separate yourselves from those who are damning themselves by their impiousness, lack of devotion, and laziness.

Without delay, make a decision to say your Rosary often with faith, humility, confidence, and perseverance.

(1) Pay serious attention to our Lord's command to pray always and consider the example that He gave us and the extreme need we have for prayer because of our darkness, ignorance, and weakness as well as the strength of our spiritual enemies.

Then you will not be satisfied with saying the Rosary once a year (as the Perpetual Members do) or once a week (as the Ordinary Members do) but will say it every day (as Members of the Daily Rosary do) and will never fail in this—even though the only obligation they have is that of saving their souls.

[137] "We ought always to pray and not lose heart" (Luke 18:1). These are the eternal words of our Lord Himself. We must believe and abide by them if we want to avoid damnation. Explain them in any way you like, as long as you do not interpret them as the world does and only observe them in a worldly way.

Our Lord gave us the true explanation of His words by the luminous examples He left us. "I have given you an example: that as I have done, so you also should do" (John 13:15). And "He spent the whole night in prayer to God" (Luke 6:12). As though His days were not long enough, He was accustomed to spend the night in prayer.

Again and again He said to His Apostles: "Watch and pray" (Matthew 26:41). The flesh is weak, and temptation is everywhere and always around you. If you do not pray constantly, you shall fall.

Some of them apparently thought these words of our Lord were only a counsel, and so they completely misunderstood. This is why they fell into temptation and sin even though they were in the company of Jesus Christ.

[138] Dear fellow member, if you want to lead a fashionable life and belong to the world—i.e., if you do not mind falling into mortal sin from time to time and then quickly going to Confession, and if you wish to avoid solely conspicuous and scandalous sins while at the same time committing "respectable sins"—there is no need for you to say so many prayers and Rosaries.

In such a case, you need to pray very little: a hasty prayer at morning and at night, an occasional Rosary that may be given to you for your penance, a few decades of Hail Marys mumbled (haphazardly and unthinkingly) when it suits your fancy to do so—this is quite enough.

If you did less, you might be branded as a libertine. If you did more, you would be dubbed a fanatic.

[139] However, if you, as a true Christian, genuinely resolved to save your soul and walk in the footsteps of the Saints, want to avoid mortal sin at all costs, escaping Satan's traps and diverting his flaming darts, you must pray always, as our Lord taught and commanded you to do.

Accordingly, you must at least say your Rosary or some equivalent prayer every day. I have said "at least" because probably all that you will accomplish through your Rosary will be to avoid mortal sin and to overcome temptation. For you are exposed to the torrents of the world's iniquity, by which many strong souls are swept away.

You are in the midst of thick darkness that often blinds the most enlightened souls and surrounded by evil spirits, who are more experienced than ever. They know their time is short and make use of all their craftiness to be successful in their temptations.

It will be a marvel of grace brought about by the Holy Rosary if you manage to avoid the blandishments of the world, the devil and the flesh, escape sin, and gain heaven.

[140] If you do not want to believe me, at least learn from your own experience!

Let me ask you: when you used to say only a few prayers and in the manner of mediocre Christians, were you able to avoid serious sins that were grievous but seeming nothing at all to you in your blindness? Hence, open your eyes, and if you want to live and die as a holy person, pray unceasingly; say your Rosary every day as members always used to do in the early days of the Confraternity.

When the Blessed Virgin gave the Holy Rosary to St. Dominic, she ordered him to say it every day and to have others say it daily. Hence, St. Dominic never let people join the Confraternity unless they were resolved to say it every day. If today people are allowed to be Ordinary Members by saying the Rosary merely once a week, it is because fervor has waned and charity has lost its ardor. You get what you can out of people who are poor in prayer, but it was not so in the beginning (see Matthew 19:8).

[141] Three things must be noted:

(a) The first is that if you want to join the Confraternity of the Daily Rosary and share in the prayers and merits of its members, it does not suffice to be enrolled in the Ordinary Rosary or only to promise to say it every day. You must also give your name to those who have the power to enroll people in it.

It is also a very good thing to go to Confession and Holy Communion, especially for this intention of joining. For the Ordinary Rosary Membership does not include the Daily Rosary Membership, but the Daily Rosary Membership does include the Ordinary Rosary Membership.

(b) The second thing to be noted is that, absolutely speaking, it is not even a venial sin to fail to say the Rosary daily, or every week, or even once a year.

(c) The third is that whenever illness, or an act of legitimate obedience, or some real necessity, or even involuntary forgetfulness has prevented you from saying your Rosary, you do not forfeit your share of the merits and your participation in the Rosaries of the other Confraternity members.

Hence, strictly speaking, you are under no obligation to say two Rosaries the next day to make up for the one you missed through no fault of your own. If, however, your sickness does not inhibit you from saying part of your Rosary, you must say that part.

"Blessed are they who stand before You always" (1 Kings 10:8). "Blessed are they who dwell in Your house. Continually they praise You" (Psalm 84:5).

"O dear Lord Jesus, blessed are the members of the Daily Rosary Confraternity who are in Your presence every day—in Your little house at Nazareth or at the foot of Your Cross on Calvary or around Your throne in heaven, intent on meditating on and contemplating Your Joyful, Sorrowful, and Glorious Mysteries. How blessed they are on earth because of the wonderful graces You deign to give them, and how blessed they shall be in heaven, where they will praise You in a very special way forever and ever!"*

[142] (2) The Rosary should be said with faith, in accord with the words of our Lord: "Everything you ask for in prayer, believe that you shall receive it, and it shall be done to you" (Mark 11:24). Believe that you will receive what you ask from the hands of Almighty God, and He will grant your petitions. He will say to you: "As you have believed, so be it

---

* This apparently is a soliloquy by St. Louis de Montfort.

done to you" (Matthew 8:13). "If any of you lacks wisdom, let him ask it of God, Who gives it . . . , but let him ask in faith, not with doubt" (James 1:5, 6), in reciting the Rosary—and he will be granted what he asks.

[143] (3) We must pray with humility like the Publican. He was kneeling on the ground on both knees, not on one knee nor with one knee on the bench in front of him, as proud and worldly people are wont to do. He was at the back of the Temple and not in the sanctuary as the Pharisee was; he had his eyes cast down, not daring to look up to heaven; neither did he hold his head up high and look about him as the Pharisee did.

He beat his breast, confessing that he was a sinner and asking forgiveness: "Be merciful to me a sinner" (Luke 18:13), and he was in no way like the Pharisee, who boasted of his good works and despised others in his prayers.

Do not imitate the haughty prayer of the Pharisee, which only hardened his heart and increased his guilt. Imitate rather the humility of the Publican in his prayer, which obtained for him the remission of his sins.

You should be very careful not to do anything out of the ordinary, nor to ask for or even desire knowledge of extraordinary things, visions, revelations, and other exceptional graces that God occasionally gives to some Saints while they are saying the Rosary. "Faith alone suffices," * now that

* A line from the Eucharistic hymn *Pange Lingua* of St. Thomas Aquinas.

the Gospels and all the devotions and pious practices have firmly been established.

At times of dryness, boredom, and interior desolation, never omit even the smallest part of your Rosary, for this would be evidence of pride and faithlessness. On the contrary, like a true champion of Jesus and Mary, you should say your Our Fathers and Hail Marys even without seeing, hearing, or feeling any consolation whatsoever, and forcing yourself to reflect as best you can on the Mysteries.

You ought not to look for candy or jam to eat with your daily bread, as children do. To more perfectly imitate our Lord in His Agony, you should even prolong your Rosary by saying it more slowly sometimes when you find it especially hard to say: "Being in an agony, He prayed the longer" (Luke 22:43), so that the same thing may be said of you that was said of our Lord: He prayed even longer.

[144] (4) Finally, pray with great confidence, based on the goodness and infinite generosity of God and on the promises of Jesus. God is a spring of living water that flows unceasingly into the hearts of those who pray. Jesus is the kindness of the Father, overflowing with every grace and virtue. The Eternal Father wants nothing so much as to share with us the life-giving waters of His grace and mercy. He cries out to us: "All you who thirst, come to the waters" (Isaiah 54:1).

This means "Come and drink of My spring through prayer," and when we do not pray to Him He says sadly that we are deserting Him: "They have deserted Me, the fountain of living water" (Jeremiah 2:13).

We make our Lord happy when we ask Him for graces. Prayer is the channel of God's grace and Christ's mercy. If we do not attain it by prayer, as is the duty of all God's children, our Lord registers a loving complaint: "Hitherto you have not asked for anything" (John 16:24). "Ask and you shall receive, seek and you shall find, knock and it shall be opened to you" (Matthew 7:7).

Furthermore, to give us more confidence in praying to Him, He has bound Himself by His word that the Father will grant us everything we ask in His name (see John 16:23).

FORTY-EIGHTH ROSE

Perseverance in Our Devotion to the Rosary

[145] (5) As a fifth point, we must join perseverance in prayer to our confidence. Only those who persevere in asking, seeking, and knocking will receive, find, and enter. It is not enough to ask God for certain graces only for a month, a year, ten or even twenty years; we must never grow weary of asking.

We must be resolute and keep on asking until the moment of death, intent on obtaining what we ask for our own salvation or die. This disposition to die must even accompany our perseverance in prayer and our trust in God, so that we can say:

"Although He should kill me, I will trust in Him"
(Job 13:15) and expect Him to give me all I ask.

[146] The generosity of prominent and rich people of the world shows itself in bestowing favors on
the needy even before the latter ask for anything.
God's munificence is shown in letting us seek and
ask over a long period of time for the graces He
wishes to give us. Indeed, quite often the more precious the grace the longer He takes to grant it—for
three reasons:

(1) To increase this grace still more in the recip-
     ient;
(2) To make the recipient appreciate it more;
(3) To make the recipient very careful not to
     lose it—for we tend not to appreciate what
     we can obtain quickly and with little effort.

Dear members of the Rosary Confraternity, persevere in asking God throughout the Rosary for all
your spiritual and corporal needs. Most of all, you
should ask for Divine Wisdom, which "is an infinite
Treasure" (Wisdom 7:14). And never doubt that you
will receive it sooner or later, so long as you do not
give up saying the Rosary and do not lose heart in
the midst of your journey: "You still have a long way
to go" (1 Kings 19:7).

You will have much adversity to face, many difficulties to overcome, and a host of enemies to conquer before you will have stored up enough treasures for eternity. You will need many Our Fathers
and Hail Marys with which to merit Paradise and
the beautiful crown that awaits each faithful Confraternity member.

"Let no one take your crown" (Revelation 3:11). Take care that your crown is not taken by somebody who has been more faithful than you in saying the daily Rosary. It was "your crown"—God had prepared it for you, and you had already won it halfway by means of the Rosaries you had said well. But then you stopped on the way, the good way on which you "were running so well" (Galatians 5:7), and so someone passed in front of you and arrived first. More diligent and faithful than you with his Rosaries and good works, he has won and paid the price to attain the crown that was yours. "Who has hindered you from following the way" (Galatians 5:7) to attain your crown? Alas, the enemies of the Holy Rosary, who are so many!

[147]   Believe me, only "the violent bear it away" (Matthew 11:12). These crowns are not for the timid who fear the world's jeers and threats. Neither are they for the lazy and slothful who only say their Rosaries carelessly, or hastily, or out of habit, or only now and then out of whim.

Nor are these crowns for cowards who lose heart and lay down their arms as soon as they see hell unloosed against their Rosary.

Dear Confraternity members, if you want to place yourselves at the service of Jesus and Mary by saying the Rosary every day, you must be prepared for temptation: "My son, when you come to the service of God, prepare your soul for temptation" (Sirach 2:1). Heretics and libertines, the so-called respectable people of the world, persons of only lukewarm piety, and false prophets, in conjunction with your fallen nature and with all the powers of hell itself, will wage fierce battles against you in an attempt to get you to forgo this holy practice.

[148] To fortify you against their attacks, not so much in the case of heretics and libertines as in the case of the respectable in the eyes of the world and the devout who do not like to say the Rosary, here are some of the things they think and say:

—*"What is it that this charlatan wants to say?"* (Acts 17:18). *"Come, let us oppress him for he is against us"* (Wisdom 2:12).

—*"Why is this person whispering so many Rosaries? What is it he is always mumbling?"*

—*"Such laziness! And what a waste of time to keep sliding those beads along! He would do much better to work instead of losing himself in this foolishness."*

—*"Yes, sure, all you have to do is to say your Rosary, and larks will come tumbling from heaven nicely roasted! The Rosary will obtain our supper for us!"*

—*"God says: Help yourself and I will help you. Why, then, do you get mixed up with so many prayers?"*

—*" 'A brief prayer pierces the heavens' (Sirach 25:20); one Our Father and Hail Mary well said are more than sufficient."*

—*"God has never ordered us to say the Rosary. Of course, it's a good thing, and even an excellent thing, when you have the time to say it. But do not think that it makes us more sure of attaining salvation. Just look at how many Saints never said it. Too many people want to make everybody see through their own eyes: those who take everything to extremes and scrupulous people who see sin everywhere, saying that all those who do not say the Rosary will go to hell."*

—*"Yes, the Rosary is all right for silly unlettered women. Why say the Rosary? Is it not better to say the Little Office of the Blessed Virgin or recite the Seven Penitential Psalms? Is there anything better than the Psalms, which are inspired by the Holy Spirit?"*

—*"You undertake to say the Rosary every day; this is nothing but a fire of straw that will not last. Would it not be better to resolve to do less and be more faithful to it?"*

—*"My friend, listen to me. Say your morning and night prayers, and work hard for God during the day. God does not ask any more of you. If you did not have a living to earn, you could bind yourself to say as many Rosaries as you wished. Therefore, say your Rosary on Sundays and Holydays, but not on weekdays when it is time to work."*

—*"Do you really want to have an enormous pair of beads in your hands? I've seen a little Rosary of only one decade, which is just as good as one of fifteen decades."*

—*"Why on earth do you want to wear the Rosary on your belt, fanatic that you are? Why don't you wear it around your neck like the Spaniards, those great sayers of the Rosary? They carry an enormous Rosary in one hand and a dagger in the other, ready to use. Get rid of these external devotions. Real devotion is in the heart, etc."*

[149] Similarly, not a few talented people and learned scholars, who are proud and self-willed, may occasionally try to dissuade you from saying the Rosary. They would rather persuade you to say the Seven Penitential Psalms or some other prayers. If a good confessor has given you a penance of saying the Rosary every day for two weeks or a month, they will tell you that all you have to do to get your penance changed to other prayers, or fasts, or Masses, or alms, is to go to one of them in confession.

If you should consult even certain people in the world who lead lives of prayer but who have no direct experience of the importance of the Rosary, they will not only not encourage it but also will turn people away from it to get them to learn contemplation—as if the Rosary and contemplation were incompatible and as if the many Saints devoted to the Rosary were not great contemplatives.

Your domestic enemies will attack you all the more cruelly because you are united with them. I mean the powers of your soul and the senses of your body, the distractions of the mind, the ennui of the will, the dryness of the heart, the weariness and illnesses of the body. All these adversaries will combine with the evil spirits and cry out to you:

—*"Stop saying your Rosary; that is what is giving you such a headache. Give it up; it is not obligatory under pain of sin. If you must say your Rosary, say only part of it. The difficulties you are having are a sign that God does not want you to say it. Better still, finish it tomorrow when you are more up to it, etc."*

[150] Dear Confraternity members, the Daily Rosary has had so many enemies that I regard the grace of persevering in it until death as one of the greatest favors God can give us.

Persevere in it, and in heaven you will have the wonderful crown that has been prepared for your fidelity: "Remain faithful until death, and I will give you the crown of life" (Revelation 2:10).

FORTY-NINTH ROSE

Observations on Indulgences*

[151] So that in saying your Rosary you may gain the indulgences that have been granted to Rosary Confraternity members, it is relevant to make some observations on indulgences.

An indulgence is the remission of the temporal punishment still owed to sins that have been forgiven in the Sacrament of Confession. The indulgence is an application of the superabundant satisfactions of Jesus Christ, of the Blessed Virgin Mary, and of the Saints that are contained in the Treasury of the Church.

A Plenary Indulgence removes all temporal punishment owed to sin; a partial indulgence, on the other hand (e.g., of a hundred or a thousand years) removes as much punishment as one would have expiated in a hundred or a thousand years if he had received penitences for such a period of time according to the ancient canons of the Church.

---

* See Appendix II, p. 239, for the Rosary Indulgences in effect today.

Let me give an example. If for a single mortal sin those canons prescribed seven years of penance (sometimes even ten or fifteen!), the punishment for twenty mortal sins would have had to be at least twenty times seven years, and so on.*

[152] Rosary Confraternity members who want to gain the indulgences must meet the following conditions:

(1) They must be truly repentant and must go to Confession and Holy Communion, as the Bull of Indulgences teaches.

(2) They must be entirely free from affection for venial sin. If such affection remains, so does the guilt and the punishment.

(3) They must say the prayers and carry out the good works designated by the Bull.
According to the mind of the Popes, partial indulgences can be aquired, e.g., for a hundred years, even if one does not gain a plenary indulgence; in such a case, it is not always necessary to go to Confession and Communion. And this holds good for indulgences annexed to the recitation of the Rosary, to possessing blessed Rosary beads, etc.

Make sure you do not neglect indulgences.

[153] Some writers tell the experience of a well-bred girl named Alexandra. She had been miraculously converted and enrolled by St. Dominic in the

---

* In his 1967 Apostolic Constitution *Indulgentiarum Doctrina*, Paul VI decreed that no specification of days or years will hereafter be attached to partial indulgences.

Confraternity of the Rosary. After her death she appeared to the Saint and said she had been sentenced to seven hundred years in purgatory because of her own sins and the sins she had influenced others to commit by her worldly ways. She begged him to ease her pains by his prayers and to ask the Confraternity members to pray for the same result. St. Dominic did what she had requested.

Fifteen days later, she reappeared to him more resplendent than the sun and telling him she had been quickly delivered from purgatory through the prayers that the Confraternity members had offered for her. She told the Saint that she had come to beg him on behalf of the Holy Souls in Purgatory to go on preaching the Rosary and to ask their relatives to offer their Rosaries for them. Then, as soon as they entered into glory, they would reward their relatives abundantly.

FIFTIETH ROSE*
Various Methods

[154] To make it easier for you to say the Holy Rosary, here are several methods that will help you recite it in a holy manner, together with meditation on the Joyful, Sorrowful, and Glorious Mysteries of Jesus and Mary. Choose the method that you like. You can also compose a method yourself, as not a few holy people have done before you.

---

* The manuscript does not have the title "Fiftieth Rose." Possibly St. Louis intended to use it for the "Methods of Saying the Rosary," which follow. Only the first two methods (nos. 1-6, pp. 171-179) are part of *The Secret of the Rosary*. The third, fourth, and fifth are found in other works by the Saint.

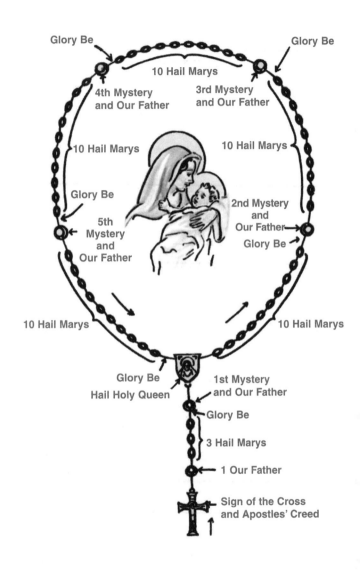

Glory Be

Glory Be

10 Hail Marys

4th Mystery
and Our Father

3rd Mystery
and Our Father

10 Hail Marys

10 Hail Marys

Glory Be

5th
Mystery
and
Our Father

2nd Mystery
and
Our Father

Glory Be

10 Hail Marys

10 Hail Marys

Glory Be
Hail Holy Queen

1st Mystery
and Our Father

Glory Be

3 Hail Marys

1 Our Father

Sign of the Cross
and Apostles' Creed

METHODS OF SAYING THE MOST HOLY ROSARY

So As To Draw Upon Our Souls the Grace of the Mysteries of the Life, Passion, and Glory of Jesus and Mary

I. First Method

Come Holy Spirit,
fill the hearts of Your faithful
and kindle in them the fire of Your love.

"O my Jesus, forgive us our sins, save us from the fire of hell, lead all souls to heaven, especially those in most need of Your mercy." *(This prayer, revealed to the three children of Fatima by the Lady of Fatima in 1917, is now added following the Glory Be to the Father at the end of each decade.)*

General Offering of the Rosary

[1] I unite myself with all the Saints in heaven, and with all the righteous on earth; I unite myself with You, my Jesus, so as to praise Your Holy Mother worthily and to praise You in her and by her. I renounce all the distractions that may come to me during this Rosary.

O Blessed Virgin Mary, we offer you this Apostles' Creed so as to honor the faith you had on earth and to ask you to have us share in the same faith.

O Lord, we offer You this Our Father to adore You in Your oneness and to recognize You as the First Cause and the Last End of all things.

Most Holy Trinity, we offer You these three Hail Marys to thank You for all the graces that You have given to Mary and all the graces that You have given us through her intercession.

1 Our Father, 3 Hail Marys, 1 Glory Be to the Father . . .

Particular Offerings for Each Decade*

The Joyful Mysteries

[2] **1st Decade:** Lord Jesus, we offer You this first decade to honor Your Incarnation, and we ask of You, through this Mystery and through the intercession of Your Holy Mother, *a deep humility of heart.*

1 Our Father, 10 Hail Marys, 1 Glory Be to the Father . . .

May the grace of the Mystery of the Incarnation come down into my soul and make it truly humble.

2nd Decade: Lord Jesus, we offer You this second decade to honor the Visitation of Your Holy Mother to her cousin St. Elizabeth, and we ask of You, through this Mystery and through the intercession of Mary, *a perfect charity toward our neighbor.*

1 Our Father, 10 Hail Marys, 1 Glory Be to the Father . . .

May the grace of the Mystery of the Visitation come down into my soul and make it truly charitable.

---

* See p. 229 for the Luminous Mysteries.

3rd Decade: Child Jesus, we offer You this third decade to honor Your Blessed Nativity, and we ask of You, through this Mystery and through the intercession of Your Holy Mother, *detachment from the things of this world, love of poverty, and love of the poor.*

1 Our Father, 10 Hail Marys, 1 Glory Be to the Father . . .

May the grace of the Mystery of the Nativity come down into my soul and make me truly poor in spirit.

4th Decade: Lord Jesus, we offer You this fourth decade to honor Your Presentation in the Temple by the hands of Mary, and we ask of You, through this Mystery and through the intercession of Your Holy Mother, *the gift of wisdom and purity of heart and body.*

1 Our Father, 10 Hail Marys, 1 Glory Be to the Father. . .

May the grace of the Mystery of the Presentation come down into my soul and make me truly wise.

5th Decade: Lord Jesus, we offer You this fifth decade to honor Your Finding in the Temple among the learned men by Mary, after she had lost You, and we ask of You, through this Mystery and through the intercession of Your Holy Mother, *our conversion as well as the conversion of all sinners, heretics, schismatics, and idolators.*

1 Our Father, 10 Hail Marys, 1 Glory Be to the Father . . .

May the grace of the Mystery of the Finding of the Child Jesus in the Temple come down into my soul and truly convert me.

The Sorrowful Mysteries

[3] **6th Decade:** Lord Jesus, we offer You this sixth decade to honor Your mortal Agony in the Garden of Olives, and we ask of You, through this Mystery and through the intercession of Your Holy Mother, *a perfect sorrow for our sins and the virtue of perfect obedience to Your Holy Will.*

1 Our Father, 10 Hail Marys, 1 Glory Be to the Father . . .

May the grace of our Lord's Agony come down into my soul and make me truly contrite and perfectly obedient to the Will of God.

7th Decade: Lord Jesus, we offer You this seventh decade to honor Your Bloody Scourging, and we ask of You, through this Mystery and through the intercession of Your Holy Mother, *the grace to mortify our senses.*

1 Our Father, 10 Hail Marys, 1 Glory Be to the Father . . .

May the grace of our Lord's Scourging come down into my soul and make me truly mortified.

8th Decade: Lord Jesus, we offer You this eighth decade to honor Your cruel Crowning with Thorns, and we ask of You, through this Mystery and through the intercession of Your Holy Mother, *a true detachment from the world.*

1 Our Father, 10 Hail Marys, 1 Glory Be to the Father . . .

May the grace of the Mystery of our Lord's Crowning with Thorns come down into my soul and make me truly detached from the world.

9th Decade: Lord Jesus, we offer You this ninth decade to honor Your Carrying of the Cross, and we ask of You, through this Mystery and through the intercession of Your Holy Mother, *great patience in carrying our cross in Your footsteps every day of our lives.*

1 Our Father, 10 Hail Marys, 1 Glory Be to the Father ...

May the grace of the Mystery of the Carrying of the Cross come down into my soul and make me truly penitent.

10th Decade: Lord Jesus, we offer You this tenth decade to honor Your Crucifixion on Mount Calvary, and we ask of You, through this Mystery and through the intercession of Your Holy Mother, *a great horror of sin, a love of the Cross, and the grace of a holy death for us and for those now in their last agony.*

1 Our Father, 10 Hail Marys, 1 Glory Be to the Father ...

May the grace of the Mystery of the Passion and Death of our Lord and Savior Jesus Christ come down into my soul and make me truly holy.

The Glorious Mysteries

[4] **11th Decade:** Lord Jesus, we offer You this eleventh decade to honor Your triumphant Resurrection, and we ask of You, through this Mystery and through the intercession of Your Holy Mother, *a living faith.*

1 Our Father, 10 Hail Marys, 1 Glory Be to the Father . . .

May the grace of the Resurrection come down into my soul and make me truly faithful.

12th Decade: Lord Jesus, we offer You this twelfth decade to honor Your glorious Ascension, and we ask of You, through this Mystery and through the intercession of Your Holy Mother, *a firm hope and a deep longing for heaven.*

1 Our Father, 10 Hail Marys, 1 Glory Be to the Father . . .

May the grace of the Mystery of the Ascension come down into my soul and make me ready for heaven.

13th Decade: Holy Spirit, we offer You this thirteenth decade to honor the Mystery of Pentecost, and we ask of You, through this Mystery and through the intercession of Mary, Your most faithful Spouse, *Your holy wisdom so that we may know, really love, and practice Your truth and make all others share in it.*

1 Our Father, 10 Hail Marys, 1 Glory Be to the Father . . .

May the grace of Pentecost come down into my soul and make me really wise in the eyes of God.

14th Decade: Lord Jesus, we offer You this fourteenth decade to honor the Immaculate Conception and Assumption of Your Holy Mother, body and soul, into heaven, and we ask of You, through these two Mysteries and through her intercession, *the gift of true devotion to her to help us live a good life and die a happy death.*

1 Our Father, 10 Hail Marys, 1 Glory Be to the Father . . .

May the grace of the Mysteries of the Immaculate Conception and the Assumption come down into my soul and make me truly devoted to Mary.

15th Decade: Lord Jesus, we offer You this fifteenth and last decade to honor the glorious Crowning of Your Holy Mother in heaven, and we ask of You, through this Mystery and through her intercession, *the grace of perseverance and increase of virtue until the very moment of death and thereafter the eternal crown that is prepared for us. We ask the same grace for all the righteous and for our benefactors.*

1 Our Father, 10 Hail Marys, 1 Glory Be to the Father . . .

May the grace of the Mystery of the Crowning of Your Holy Mother in heaven come down into my soul and make me increase in perseverance and virtue.

[5] We beseech You, dear Lord Jesus, through the fifteen Mysteries of Your Life, Passion, Death and Glory, and through the merits of Your Holy Mother, to convert sinners, help the dying, deliver the Holy Souls from purgatory, and give all of us Your grace, so that we may live well and die a holy death. And please, give us the Light of Your glory later on so that we may see You face to face and love You for all eternity. Amen.

II. Second and Shorter Method

A Shorter Way of Commemorating the Life, Death, and Glory of Jesus and Mary in Reciting the Holy Rosary and Lessening the Distraction of the Imagination

[6]   To do this we must add a word or two to each Hail Mary of every decade that reminds us of the Mystery being celebrated. This word or words should be added after the name "Jesus" halfway through the prayer: "and blessed is the fruit of your womb . . ."

1st Decade: . . . and blessed is the fruit of your womb "Jesus incarnate."

2nd Decade: . . . and blessed is the fruit of your womb "Jesus Who sanctifies."

3rd Decade: . . . and blessed is the fruit of your womb "Jesus born in poverty."

4th Decade: . . . and blessed is the fruit of your womb "Jesus offered for us."

5th Decade: . . . and blessed is the fruit of your womb "Jesus, the Saint of Saints."

6th Decade: . . . and blessed is the fruit of your womb "Jesus in His agony."

7th Decade: . . . and blessed is the fruit of your womb "Jesus Scourged."

8th Decade: . . . and blessed is the fruit of your womb "Jesus Crowned with Thorns."

9th Decade: . . . and blessed is the fruit of your womb "Jesus Carrying His Cross."

10th Decade: . . . and blessed is the fruit of your womb "Jesus Crucified."

11th Decade: . . . and blessed is the fruit of your womb "Jesus risen from the dead."

12th Decade: . . . and blessed is the fruit of your womb "Jesus ascending to heaven."

13th Decade: . . . and blessed is the fruit of your womb "Jesus filling you [Mary] with the Holy Spirit."

14th Decade: . . . and blessed is the fruit of your womb "Jesus raising you up."

15th Decade: . . . and blessed is the fruit of your womb "Jesus crowning you with glory."*

At the end of the first five Mysteries, we say:

May the grace of the Joyful Mysteries come down into our souls and make us really holy.

At the end of the second five:

May the grace of the Sorrowful Mysteries come down into our souls and make us truly patient.

At the end of the third five:

May the grace of the Glorious Mysteries come down into our souls and make us eternally happy. Amen.

---

* See p. 229 for the Luminous Mysteries.

*III. Third Method**

For Use of the Daughters of Wisdom In Saying the Holy Rosary Fruitfully

[7] I unite myself with all the Angels in heaven, all the righteous on earth, and all the faithful who live in this place. I unite myself with You, Lord Jesus, in order to praise Your Holy Mother worthily and to praise You in her and with her.

I renounce the distractions that will come upon me during this Rosary, which I intend to say with recollection, attention, and devotion, as if it were the last day of my life. R̹. Amen.

Lord Jesus, we offer You the Creed to honor all the Mysteries of the Faith; the Our Father and Hail Mary to honor God in the Unity of nature and in the Trinity of persons. We ask of You a living faith, a firm hope, and an ardent love. R̹. Amen.

At every Mystery after the words: "Blessed is the fruit of your womb, Jesus," add a word or phrase to recall and honor the particular Mystery. For example, "Jesus incarnate," "Jesus Who sanctifies," etc., as indicated at every decade.

---

* As already noted, the third, fourth, and fifth Methods are not in the manuscript of St. Louis's *Secret of the Rosary* but come from elsewhere in his writings. They are added here to round out the Saint's methods for our readers.

The Joyful Mysteries*

The Incarnation

[8] Lord Jesus, we offer You this first decade to honor Your Incarnation in Mary's womb, and we ask of You, through this Mystery and through her intercession, *a deep humility.* ℞. Amen.

1 Our Father. 10 Hail Marys, with the addition: *"Jesus becoming man."*

May the graces of the Mystery of the Incarnation come down into our souls. ℞. Amen.

The Visitation

Lord Jesus, we offer You this second decade to honor the Visitation of Your Holy Mother to her cousin St. Elizabeth and the sanctification of St. John the Baptist, and we ask of You, through this Mystery and through her intercession, *love for our neighbor.* ℞. Amen.

1 Our Father, 10 Hail Marys . . . "Jesus Who sanctifies."

May the graces of the Mystery of the Visitation come down into our souls. ℞. Amen.

The Birth of Jesus

Lord Jesus, we offer You this third decade to honor Your Birth in the stable at Bethlehem, and we ask of You, through this Mystery and through the intercession of Your Holy Mother, *detachment from worldly goods, disinterest in riches, and love of poverty.* ℞. Amen.

---

* See p. 229 for the Luminous Mysteries.

1 Our Father, 10 Hail Marys . . . "Jesus, born of Mary."

May the graces of the Birth of Jesus come down into our souls. ℟. Amen.

The Presentation in the Temple

Lord Jesus, we offer You this fourth decade to honor Your Presentation in the Temple and the Purification of Mary, and we ask of You, through this Mystery and through her intercession, *a great purity of body and soul.* ℟. Amen.

1 Our Father, 10 Hail Marys . . . "Jesus offered in sacrifice."

May the graces of the Mystery of the Presentation come down into our souls. ℟. Amen.

The Finding of Jesus

Lord Jesus, we offer You this fifth decade to honor Your Finding in the Temple by Mary, and we ask of You, through this Mystery and through her intercession, *true wisdom.* ℟. Amen.

1 Our Father, 10 Hail Marys . . . "Jesus, the Saint of Saints."

May the graces of the Mystery of the Finding of Jesus come down into our souls. ℟. Amen.

At the end of this first chaplet, the Magnificat *is said.*

The Sorrowful Mysteries

The Agony

[9] Lord Jesus, we offer You this sixth decade to honor Your mortal Agony in the Garden of Olives,

and we ask of You, through this Mystery and through the intercession of Your Holy Mother, *sorrow for our sins.* ℟. Amen.

1 Our Father, 10 Hail Marys . . . "Jesus in Agony."

May the graces of the Agony of Jesus come down into our souls. ℟. Amen.

The Scourging

Lord Jesus, we offer You this seventh decade to honor Your bloody Scourging, and we ask of You, through this Mystery and through the intercession of Your Holy Mother, *the mortification of our senses.* ℟. Amen.

1 Our Father, 10 Hail Marys . . . "Jesus scourged."

May the graces of the Mystery of the Scourging of Jesus come down into our souls. ℟. Amen.

The Crowning with Thorns

Lord Jesus, we offer You this eighth decade to honor Your Crowning with Thorns, and we ask of You, through this Mystery and through the intercession of Your Holy Mother, *detachment from the spirit of the world.* ℟. Amen.

1 Our Father, 10 Hail Marys . . . "Jesus crowned with thorns."

May the graces of the Mystery of the Crowning with Thorns come down into our souls. ℟. Amen.

The Carrying of the Cross

Lord Jesus, we offer You this ninth decade to honor Your Carrying of the Cross to Calvary, and we ask of You, through this Mystery and through the intercession of Your Holy Mother, *constancy in carrying our crosses.* ℟. Amen.

1 Our Father, 10 Hail Marys . . . "Jesus carrying His Cross."

May the graces of the Mystery of Jesus carrying His Cross come down into our souls. ℟. Amen.

The Crucifixion

Lord Jesus, we offer You this tenth decade to honor Your Crucifixion and cruel Death on Calvary, and we ask of You, through this Mystery and through the intercession of Your Holy Mother, *conversion for sinners, perseverance for the righteous, and rest for the souls in purgatory.* ℟. Amen.

1 Our Father, 10 Hail Marys . . . "Jesus crucified."

May the graces of the Mystery of Jesus' Crucifixion come down into our souls. ℟. Amen.

[10] In this decade of the Rosary, before every Hail Mary, we ask of God, through the intercession of the nine choirs of Angels, the graces that we need:

Holy Seraphim, ask of God . . . Hail Mary . . .
Holy Cherubim, ask of God . . . Hail Mary . . .
Holy Thrones, ask of God . . . Hail Mary . . .
Holy Dominations, ask of God . . . Hail Mary . . .
Holy Virtues, ask of God . . . Hail Mary . . .
Holy Powers, ask of God . . . Hail Mary . . .
Holy Principalities, ask of God . . . Hail Mary . . .
Holy Archangels, ask of God . . . Hail Mary . . .
Holy Angels, ask of God . . . Hail Mary . . .
All the Saints of Paradise, ask of God . . . Hail Mary . . . Glory Be to the Father . . .

[11] *At the end of this second chaplet, the following prayers are said kneeling.*

Prayer
Composed by St. Louis de Montfort
To Ask and Obtain Divine Wisdom from God

God of our fathers,
merciful Lord,
Spirit of truth,
I, a poor creature,
prostrate before Your Divine Majesty,
am aware of finding myself in great need
of Your Divine Wisdom,
which I have lost by my sins.
Trusting that You will faithfully keep
Your promise to give Wisdom
to all who ask You for it
without hesitation,
I now ask it of You
with lively insistence and profound humility.
Send us, O Lord, this Wisdom,
which is ever present before Your throne
and contains all Your benefits.
It strengthens our weakness,
enlightens our minds,
inflames our hearts,
teaches us to speak and act,
to work and suffer
with You.
Direct our footsteps and calm our souls
with the virtues of Jesus Christ
and the gifts of the Holy Spirit.

Merciful Father,
God of all consolation,
through the motherly goodness of Mary,
through the Precious Blood of Your beloved Son,
through Your immense desire
to bestow Your gifts on creatures,
we ask of You the infinite treasure
of Your Wisdom.
Hear and answer this prayer of ours.
℟. Amen.

Prayer to St. Joseph

[12] Hail Joseph, a just man, Wisdom is with you. Blessed are you among men and blessed is the fruit of Mary your faithful spouse, Jesus.

Holy Joseph, worthy foster father of Jesus, pray for us sinners and obtain Divine Wisdom for us, now and at the hour of our death. ℟. Amen.

This prayer is said three times.

The Glorious Mysteries

The Resurrection

[13] Lord Jesus, we offer You this eleventh decade to honor Your glorious Resurrection, and we ask of You, through this Mystery and through the intercession of Your Holy Mother, *love for God and a joyous fidelity to His service.* ℟. Amen.

1 Our Father, 10 Hail Marys . . . "Jesus risen."

May the graces of the Mystery of the Resurrection come down into our souls. ℟. Amen.

The Ascension

Lord Jesus, we offer You this twelfth decade to honor Your triumphal Ascension, and we ask of You, through this Mystery and through the intercession of Your Holy Mother, *an ardent desire for heaven, our homeland.* ℟. Amen.

1 Our Father, 10 Hail Marys . . . "Jesus ascended into heaven."

May the graces of the Mystery of the Ascension come down into our souls. ℟. Amen.

Pentecost

Lord Jesus, we offer You this thirteenth decade to honor the Mystery of Pentecost, and we ask of You, through this Mystery and through the intercession of Your Holy Mother, *the coming of the Holy Spirit into our souls.* ℟. Amen.

1 Our Father, 10 Hail Marys . . . "Jesus Who fills you with the Holy Spirit."

May the graces of the Mystery of Pentecost come down into our souls. ℟. Amen.

The Assumption of Mary

Lord Jesus, we offer You this fourteenth decade to honor the Resurrection and triumphal Assumption into heaven of Your Holy Mother, and we ask of You, through this Mystery and through her intercession, *filial affection for such a good Mother.* ℟. Amen.

1 Our Father, 10 Hail Marys . . . "Jesus Who makes you conquer death."

May the graces of the Mystery of Mary's Assumption come down into our souls. ℟. Amen.

The Crowning of Mary

Lord Jesus, we offer You this fifteenth and last decade to honor the Crowning of Your Holy Mother, and we ask of You, through this Mystery and through her intercession, *perseverance in grace and the crown of glory.* ℟. Amen.

1 Our Father, 10 Hail Marys . . . "Jesus Who crowns you in glory."

May the graces of the Mystery of Mary's Crowning come down into our souls. ℟. Amen.

[14] In this decade of the Rosary, before every Hail Mary, we ask of God, through the intercession of all the Saints, the graces that we need:

St. Michael the Archangel and all the holy Angels, ask of God . . . Hail Mary . . .

Saint Abraham and all the Patriarchs, ask of God . . . Hail Mary . . .

St. John the Baptist and all the holy Prophets, ask of God . . . Hail Mary . . .

St. Peter and St. Paul and all the holy Apostles, ask of God . . . Hail Mary . . .

St. Stephen, St. Lawrence, and all the holy Martyrs, ask of God . . . Hail Mary . . .

St. Hilary and all the holy Bishops, ask of God . . . Hail Mary . . .

St. Joseph and all the holy Confessors, ask of God . . . Hail Mary . . .

Saint Catherine, St. Teresa, and all the holy Virgins, ask of God . . . Hail Mary . . .

St. Anne and all the holy Women, ask of God . . .
Hail Mary . . .

Glory Be to the Father . . .

May the graces of the Mystery of the Crowning of Mary come down into our souls. ℞. Amen.

[15] *At the end of the third chaplet, the following prayer is added.*

Prayer to the Blessed Virgin Mary

I greet you, Mary, favored Daughter of the eternal Father,
admirable Mother of the Son,
faithful Spouse of the Holy Spirit,
and living Temple of the Most Holy Trinity.
I greet you, sovereign Queen.
Subject to you is everything
in heaven and on earth.
I greet you, secure Refuge of sinners
and merciful Queen.
You never reject anyone.
As a sinner I throw myself at your feet
and beg you to obtain for me from Your beloved Son Jesus
contrition and sorrow for all my sins
together with Divine Wisdom.
I give myself wholly to you with all that I have,
and I choose you today as my Mother and Queen.
Hence, treat me as the last of your children
and the most lowly of your servants.
Hear, O my Queen, the sighs of my heart
that seeks to love and serve you faithfully.

Do not let it be said that
among all those who have had recourse to you
I am the first who was not heard.
O my hope and my life!
O faithful and Immaculate Virgin Mary!
Hear, defend, and strengthen me;
instruct and save me!
℟. Amen.

Praised, adored, and loved
may be Jesus in the Most Holy Sacrament of the
     Altar.
℟. Now and forever.

O Jesus, dear Jesus!
O Mary, Mother of Jesus and our Mother!
Give us your holy blessing.
℟. Amen.

Sustain us in our weaknesses,
hear us in our prayers,
and defend us from the world and the devil.
℟. Amen.

May the Virgin Mary bless us her devout chil-
     dren.
℟. Amen.

IV. Fourth Method

Summary of the Life, Passion, Death, and Glory of Jesus and of Mary in the Holy Rosary

[16] *Creed:* (1) faith in the presence of God; (2) faith in the Gospel; (3) faith and obedience to the Pope as the Vicar of Christ.

Our Father: unity of one living and true God.

1st Hail Mary: to honor the eternal Father Who generates the Son in contemplating Himself.

2nd Hail Mary: to honor the eternal Word Who is equal to the Father and from Whose mutual love, as from a single principle, the Holy Spirit proceeds.

3rd Hail Mary: to honor the Holy Spirit Who proceeds from the Father and from the Son by way of love.

The Incarnation

[17] *Our Father:* the immense love of God.

1st Hail Mary: to express sorrow for the unhappy state of disobedient Adam, for his condemnation, and for that of his descendants.

2nd Hail Mary: to honor the desires of the Patriarchs and Prophets who prayed for the coming of the Messiah.

3rd Hail Mary: to honor the elevated desires and prayers of the Blessed Virgin to hasten the coming of the Messiah, and to honor her marriage to Joseph.

4th Hail Mary: the love of the eternal Father Who has given us His own Son.

5th Hail Mary: the love of the Son Who has given Himself for us.

6th Hail Mary: the sending and the salutation of the Angel Gabriel.

7th Hail Mary: the virginal fear of Mary.

8th Hail Mary: the faith and the consent of the Blessed Virgin.

9th Hail Mary: the creation of the soul and body of Jesus Christ in the womb of Mary by the Holy Spirit.

10th Hail Mary: the adoration by the Angels of the Word Incarnate in the womb of Mary.

The Visitation

[18] *Our Father:* the most adorable Majesty of God.

1st Hail Mary: to honor the joy of the heart of Mary at the Incarnation and the nine-month stay of the Incarnate Word in her womb.

2nd Hail Mary: the sacrificial offering that Jesus Christ made of Himself to the Father when coming into the world.

3rd Hail Mary: the delights of Jesus Christ in the humble and virginal womb of Mary, and those of Mary in the enjoyment of her God.

4th Hail Mary: the ambivalence of St. Joseph about the pregnancy of Mary.

5th Hail Mary: the choice of the elect agreed upon by Jesus and Mary in her virginal womb.

6th Hail Mary: the solicitude of Mary in her visit to Elizabeth.

7th Hail Mary: Mary's greeting and the sanctification of John the Baptist and his mother Elizabeth.

8th Hail Mary: the gratitude of Mary in her encounters with God expressed in the *Magnificat*.

9th Hail Mary: Mary's charity and humility in serving her cousin.

10th Hail Mary: the mutual dependence of Jesus and Mary and our dependence on them.

The Birth of Jesus

[19] *Our Father:* the infinite riches of God.

1st Hail Mary: to honor the rejection and the humiliations endured by Mary and Joseph at Bethlehem.

2nd Hail Mary: the poverty of the stable in which God came to the world.

3rd Hail Mary: the lofty contemplation and immense love of Mary at the moment when she was about to bring forth the Son to the world.

4th Hail Mary: the virginal birth of the eternal Word.

5th Hail Mary: the adorations and the songs of the Angels at the birth of Jesus.

6th Hail Mary: the enchanting beauty of Mary's Divine Child.

7th Hail Mary: the coming of the shepherds to the stable with their little gifts.

8th Hail Mary: the circumcision of Jesus and how much He suffered out of love.

9th Hail Mary: the imposition of the name Jesus and its greatness.

10th Hail Mary: the adoration of the Magi, and their gifts.

The Purification

[20] *Our Father:* the eternal Wisdom of God.

1st Hail Mary: to honor the obedience of Jesus and Mary to the Law.

2nd Hail Mary: the sacrifice that Jesus offered of His Humanity in this Mystery.

3rd Hail Mary: the sacrifice that the Blessed Virgin offered of her reputation.

4th Hail Mary: the joy and the canticles of Simeon and Anna the prophetess.

5th Hail Mary: the ransoming of Jesus with the offering of two turtledoves.

6th Hail Mary: the massacre of the Holy Innocents because of the cruelty of Herod.

7th Hail Mary: the flight of Jesus into Egypt through the obedience of St. Joseph to the word of an Angel.

8th Hail Mary: His mysterious stay in Egypt.

9th Hail Mary: the return of Jesus to Nazareth.

10th Hail Mary: His growth in age and wisdom.

The Finding of Jesus in the Temple

[21] *Our Father:* the unfathomable holiness of God.

1st Hail Mary: to honor Christ's Hidden Life at Nazareth filled with hard work and obedience.

2nd Hail Mary: His preaching and His Finding among the Doctors in the Temple.

3rd Hail Mary: His fasting and temptation in the desert.

4th Hail Mary: His Baptism at the hands of St. John the Baptist.

5th Hail Mary: His wondrous preaching.

6th Hail Mary: His stupendous miracles.

7th Hail Mary: the selection of the Twelve Apostles and the powers given them.

8th Hail Mary: Jesus' wonderful Transfiguration.

9th Hail Mary: His washing of the Apostles' feet.

10th Hail Mary: the institution of the Eucharist.

The Agony of Jesus Christ

[22] *Our Father:* the intimate happiness of God.

1st Hail Mary: to honor Christ's moments of contemplation during His Life and especially in the Garden of Olives.

2nd Hail Mary: His humble and fervent prayers during His Life and especially on the eve of His Passion.

3rd Hail Mary: His patience and tenderness toward the Apostles during His Life and especially in the Garden of Olives.

4th Hail Mary: the sorrows experienced in His soul during His Life, and especially in the Garden of Olives.

5th Hail Mary: the bloody sweat flowing from His sorrows.

6th Hail Mary: the consolation He deigned to accept from an Angel.

7th Hail Mary: the conformity of His will to that of His Father in spite of the aversion of nature.

8th Hail Mary: the courage with which He approached His executioners and the power of His word by which He rendered them prostrate on the ground and then uplifted them.

9th Hail Mary: His betrayal by Judas and His arrest by the Jews.

10th Hail Mary: His abandonment by the Apostles.

The Scourging

[23] *Our Father:* the wondrous patience of God.

1st Hail Mary: to honor the chains and ropes with which Jesus was bound.

2nd Hail Mary: the slap that He received in the house of Caiaphas.

3rd Hail Mary: Peter's threefold denial.

4th Hail Mary: the humiliations endured by Jesus at the hands of Herod when He was made to wear a white robe.

5th Hail Mary: Jesus stripped of His clothes.

6th Hail Mary: the scorn and insults He received from His executioners because of His nakedness.

7th Hail Mary: the sharp rods and ruthless whips with which He was beaten and tortured.

8th Hail Mary: the pillar to which He was tied.

9th Hail Mary: the blood He shed and the injuries He received in His flesh.

10th Hail Mary: His collapse out of weakness into a puddle of His own blood.

The Crowning with Thorns

[24] *Our Father:* the ineffable beauty of God.

1st Hail Mary: to honor Jesus undressed for a third time.

2nd Hail Mary: the crown of thorns.

3rd Hail Mary: the veil with which His eyes were blindfolded.

4th Hail Mary: the blows endured and the spittle from those whom He could not see.

5th Hail Mary: the old robe that was thrown around His shoulders.

6th Hail Mary: the reed that they thrust in His hand.

7th Hail Mary: the sharp stone on which He was forced to sit.

8th Hail Mary: the abuses and insults that were directed at Him.

9th Hail Mary: the blood that flowed from His adorable head.

10th Hail Mary: His hair and beard that were torn.

The Way of the Cross

[25] *Our Father:* the infinite power of God.

1st Hail Mary: to honor the presentation of our Lord to the people with the words: "Behold, the Man!"

2nd Hail Mary: the choice given to Barabbas over Jesus.

3rd Hail Mary: the false accusations made against Him.

4th Hail Mary: His condemnation to death.

5th Hail Mary: the love with which Jesus embraced the Cross and kissed it.

6th Hail Mary: the horrific pains that He endured in carrying it.

7th Hail Mary: the falls of a weakened Jesus under the weight of the Cross.

8th Hail Mary: His sorrowful meeting with His Holy Mother.

9th Hail Mary: the veil of Veronica on which He left an imprint of His countenance.

10th Hail Mary: the tears of Jesus, as well as those of His Mother and the pious women who followed Him to Calvary.

The Crucifixion of Jesus Christ

[26] *Our Father:* the fearful justice of God.

1st Hail Mary: to honor the five wounds of Jesus Christ and the blood He shed on the Cross.

2nd Hail Mary: His pierced heart and the Cross to which He was nailed.

3rd Hail Mary: the nails and the lance that pierced Him, the sponge with the myrrh and vinegar that were offered to Him to drink.

4th Hail Mary: the shame and disgrace that He experienced at being crucified naked between two robbers.

5th Hail Mary: the compassion of His Holy Mother.

6th Hail Mary: His seven last words.

7th Hail Mary: His feeling of abandonment and His silence.

8th Hail Mary: the distress of the entire universe.

9th Hail Mary: His cruel and infamous Death.

10th Hail Mary: His taking down from the Cross and burial.

The Resurrection

[27] *Our Father:* the eternity of God.

1st Hail Mary: to honor the descent of the soul of our Lord into hell.

2nd Hail Mary: the joy of the fathers and their release from limbo.

3rd Hail Mary: the reunion of the soul and body of Jesus in the tomb.

4th Hail Mary: His miraculous rise from the tomb.

5th Hail Mary: His victory over death, sin, the world, and the devil.

6th Hail Mary: the four qualities of His glorious body.

7th Hail Mary: the power that he received from His Father in heaven and on earth.

8th Hail Mary: His risen appearances with which He honored His Holy Mother, the Apostles, and the disciples.

9th Hail Mary: His discourses about heaven and the meal that He took with the disciples.

10th Hail Mary: the peace, authority, and mission that He gave to the Apostles to go out into the entire world.

The Ascension

[28] *Our Father:* the unlimited immensity of God.

1st Hail Mary: to honor the promise that Jesus gave to the Apostles that He would send them the Holy Spirit as well as the command He gave them to prepare themselves to receive Him.

2nd Hail Mary: the reunion and assembly of all His disciples on the Mount of Olives.

3rd Hail Mary: the blessing imparted to them by Jesus as He was rising from the earth to heaven.

4th Hail Mary: His glorious and delightful Ascension into heaven by virtue of His own power.

5th Hail Mary: the welcome and Divine triumph with which He was received by His Father and by the whole celestial assembly.

6th Hail Mary: the glorious power with which Jesus threw open the gates of heaven, through which no mortal had ever passed.

7th Hail Mary: the enthronement of Jesus at the right hand of the Father as His beloved Son, equal to Him.

8th Hail Mary: the power He received to judge the living and the dead.

9th Hail Mary: His final coming on earth when His power and His majesty will appear in all their splendor.

10th Hail Mary: the justice that He will exercise in the Final Judgment, rewarding the good and punishing the wicked for all eternity.

Pentecost

[29] *Our Father:* the universal providence of God.

1st Hail Mary: to honor the truth of God the Holy Spirit, Who proceeds from the Father and from the Son and is the heart of the Trinity.

2nd Hail Mary: the sending of the Holy Spirit upon the Apostles by the Father and the Son.

3rd Hail Mary: the force with which He came, a sign of His strength and power.

4th Hail Mary: the tongues of fire sent upon the Apostles to infuse in them the understanding of the Scriptures as well as the love of God and neighbor.

5th Hail Mary: the fullness of grace with which He gifted the heart of Mary, His faithful Spouse.

6th Hail Mary: His wonderful action on all the Saints and on the person of Jesus Christ, Whom He guided throughout His Life.

7th Hail Mary: the twelve fruits of the Holy Spirit.

8th Hail Mary: the seven gifts of the Holy Spirit.

9th Hail Mary: to ask for in particular the gift of Wisdom and the coming of His Kingdom in people's hearts.

10th Hail Mary: to obtain the victory over the three wicked spirits opposed to Him: the spirits of the flesh, the world, and the devil.

The Assumption of Mary

[30] *Our Father:* the inexpressible generosity of God.

1st Hail Mary: to honor the eternal predestination of Mary to be the masterpiece of God's handiwork.

2nd Hail Mary: her immaculate conception and her fullness of grace and understanding from the very womb of her mother St. Anne.

3rd Hail Mary: her birth that gave joy to the whole world.

4th Hail Mary: her presentation and her dwelling in the Temple.

5th Hail Mary: her wonderful life that was free of all sin.

6th Hail Mary: the fullness of her singular virtues.

7th Hail Mary: her fruitful virginity and her childbearing without pain.

8th Hail Mary: her Divine Motherhood and her alliance with the Blessed Trinity.

9th Hail Mary: her precious death out of love.

10th Hail Mary: her triumphal resurrection and assumption.

The Crowning of Mary

[31]   *Our Father:* the inaccessible glory of God.

1st Hail Mary: to honor the threefold crown with which Mary was invested by the Blessed Trinity.

2nd Hail Mary: the increase of joy and glory brought to heaven by her triumph.

3rd Hail Mary: to acknowledge her as Queen of heaven and earth, of Angels and human beings.

4th Hail Mary: treasurer and dispensatrix of the graces of God, the merits of Jesus Christ, and the gifts of the Holy Spirit.

5th Hail Mary: mediatrix and advocate of human beings.

6th Hail Mary: exterminator and ruin of the devil and of heresies.

7th Hail Mary: secure refuge of sinners.

8th Hail Mary: nursing Mother of Christians.

9th Hail Mary: joy and sweetness of the righteous.

10th Hail Mary: universal refuge of the living and all-powerful consolation of the afflicted, the dying, and the souls in purgatory.

V. Fifth Method

150 Reasons That Induce Us
To Say the Rosary

[32] *Creed:* definition and essence of the Holy Rosary.

1st Our Father: distinctiveness of the Rosary.

1st Hail Mary: daily Rosary.

2nd Hail Mary: ordinary Rosary.

3rd Hail Mary: perpetual Rosary.

[33] *2nd Our Father:* excellence of the Holy Rosary as indicated by the figures of the Old Testament and by the parables of the New.

1st Hail Mary: its strength against the world as indicated by the figure of the small stone that without human intervention fell upon the statue of Nebuchadnezzar and shattered it.

2nd Hail Mary: its efficacy against the devil as indicated by the figure of the sling with which David defeated Goliath.

3rd Hail Mary: its power against every kind of enemy of salvation as indicated by the figure of the tower of David, in which there were countless types of offensive and defensive weapons.

4th Hail Mary: its prodigies as prefigured by the rod of Moses that brought forth water from the rock, calmed the waters, divided the seas, and worked many other prodigies.

5th Hail Mary: its holiness as indicated by the figure of the Ark of the Covenant that contained the Law, the manna, and the rod as well as by the Psalter of David that prefigured the Rosary.

6th Hail Mary: its light as indicated by the column of fire during the night and by the luminous cloud during the day that guided the Israelites.

7th Hail Mary: its sweetness as indicated by the honey found in the mouth of a lion.

8th Hail Mary: its fruitfulness as indicated by the net that St. Peter cast into the water at the Lord's command and that did not break under the weight of 153 fish.

9th Hail Mary: its marvelous fruit as indicated by the parable of the mustard seed, which although small in appearance becomes a great tree in which the birds of the sky build their nests.

10th Hail Mary: its riches as indicated by the treasure hidden in a field, for which a wise man will give up all he possesses.

[34] *3rd Our Father:* the Rosary is a gift come down from heaven and a perfect present that God offers to His most faithful servants.

1st Hail Mary: God is the author of the prayers that comprise it and the Mysteries that it contains.

2nd Hail Mary: the Blessed Virgin is the one who fashioned the Rosary.

3rd Hail Mary: although Dominic was a Saint, he initially converted hardly any sinners.

4th Hail Mary: he was accompanied by several holy Bishops in his missions, but his efforts remained fruitless.

5th Hail Mary: after many prayers and penances, he obtained the gift of the Rosary in the forest of Toulouse.

6th Hail Mary: entering Toulouse, he preached the Rosary there and achieved resounding success and great blessings.

7th Hail Mary: he continued to preach the Rosary all his life with immense fruits.

8th Hail Mary: the marvelous effects that the Rosary produced wherever it was preached.

9th Hail Mary: the decline of the Rosary.

10th Hail Mary: its restoration at the hands of Blessed Alan de la Roche.

[35] *4th Our Father:* the Rosary is the threefold crown that is placed on the heads of Jesus and Mary and that will be placed on the head of everyone who recites it daily.

1st Hail Mary: the Blessed Virgin possesses three kinds of crowns.

2nd Hail Mary: the daily Rosary is her great crown.

3rd Hail Mary: the reprobate crown themselves with wilted roses.

4th Hail Mary: the predestined crown Jesus and Mary with eternal roses.

5th Hail Mary: His torturers* crown Jesus with sharp thorns.

6th Hail Mary: true Christians crown Him with fragrant roses.

---

* The original reads: "the Jews."

7th Hail Mary: with the first part of the Rosary [i.e., the Joyful Mysteries], we place on Mary's head the first or bridal crown, the crown of excellence.

8th Hail Mary: with the second part [i.e., the Sorrowful Mysteries], we place on her head the second or triumphal crown, the crown of power.

9th Hail Mary: with the third part [i.e., the Glorious Mysteries], we place on her head the third or royal crown, the crown of goodness.

10th Hail Mary: there are three crowns for one who recites the daily Rosary: the crown of graces in this life, the crown of peace at death, and the crown of glory in eternity.

[36] *5th Our Father:* the Rosary is the mystical summary of the most beautiful prayers of the Church.

1st Hail Mary: the Creed is the summary of the Gospel.

2nd Hail Mary: it is the prayer of the faithful.

3rd Hail Mary: it is the shield of the soldiers of Jesus Christ.

4th Hail Mary: the Our Father is the prayer that has Jesus Christ as its author.

5th Hail Mary: it is the prayer with which He had recourse to His Father and obtained whatever He desired.

6th Hail Mary: it is the prayer that contains as many Mysteries as words.

7th Hail Mary: it is the prayer that contains all our duties toward God.

8th Hail Mary: it is the prayer that summarizes everything that we should ask of God.

9th Hail Mary: it is the prayer that is not well known to the majority of Christians and said badly by them.

10th Hail Mary: paraphrase of the Our Father.

[37] *6th Our Father:* the Rosary contains the Angelic Salutation, i.e., the most pleasing prayer that one can address to Mary.

1st Hail Mary: the Hail Mary is the Divine compliment that conquers the heart of Mary.

2nd Hail Mary: it is the new song of the New Testament that the faithful sing as they are set free from slavery to the devil.

3rd Hail Mary: it is the song of the Angels and the Saints in heaven.

4th Hail Mary: it is the prayer of the predestinate and of Catholics.

5th Hail Mary: it is a mystical rose that brings joy to the Blessed Virgin and to the soul.

6th Hail Mary: it is a precious stone that adorns and sanctifies the soul.

7th Hail Mary: it is the price that enables us to purchase heaven.

8th Hail Mary: it is the prayer that distinguishes the predestinate from the reprobate.

9th Hail Mary: it is the terror of the devil, the blow that overcomes him, the nail of Sisera that pierces his head.

10th Hail Mary: paraphrase of the Hail Mary.

[38] *7th Our Father:* the Rosary is the Divine summary of the Mysteries of Jesus and Mary that recall the Life, Passion, and Glory of each of them.

1st Hail Mary: the evils and ruin of human beings stem from their ignorance and neglect of the Mysteries of Jesus Christ.

2nd Hail Mary: the Rosary enables us to know and recall the Mysteries of Jesus and Mary so that we may apply them to our lives.

3rd Hail Mary: the most lively desire of Jesus Christ was and still is that we might remember Him; for this purpose He instituted the Eucharist.

4th Hail Mary: after the Holy Mass, the Rosary is the most holy prayer and action that we can perform since it is the memorial and celebration of what Jesus Christ has done and suffered for us.

5th Hail Mary: the Rosary is the prayer of the Angels and Saints in heaven: they continuously celebrate the Life, Death, and Glory of Jesus Christ.

6th Hail Mary: by reciting the Rosary we celebrate in one day or in one week all the Divine Mysteries that the Church celebrates throughout the year for the sanctification of her faithful.

7th Hail Mary: those who recite the Rosary daily participate in what the Saints do in heaven as if they were still on earth and capable of gaining merit, for the faithful do on earth what the Saints do in heaven.

8th Hail Mary: the Mysteries of the Rosary are like mirrors in which the predestinate see their defects and like torches that guide them through the darkness of the earth.

9th Hail Mary: they are fountains of living water from the Savior in which we can joyously attain the saving waters of grace.

10th Hail Mary: they are the fifteen steps of the Temple of Solomon and the fifteen rungs of the ladder of Jacob on which the Angels come down to the predestinate and with them ascend to heaven.

[39] *8th Our Father:* the Rosary is the tree of life that bears abundant fruit all year round.

1st Hail Mary: the Rosary enlightens unseeing and hardened sinners.

2nd Hail Mary: it converts obstinate heretics.

3rd Hail Mary: it sets prisoners free.

4th Hail Mary: it heals the sick.

5th Hail Mary: it enriches the poor.

6th Hail Mary: it sustains the weak.

7th Hail Mary: it comforts the afflicted and the dying.

8th Hail Mary: it reforms religious orders that have become lukewarm.

9th Hail Mary: it holds back the scourges of the Divine anger.

10th Hail Mary: it makes the righteous perfect.

[40] *9th Our Father:* the Rosary is a prayer sanctioned by God through countless miracles.

1st Hail Mary: miracles for the conversion of sinners.

2nd Hail Mary: for the conversion of heretics.

3rd Hail Mary: for the healing of all kinds of infirmity.

4th Hail Mary: for brethren who are dying.

5th Hail Mary: for the sanctification of the devout.

6th Hail Mary: for the release of souls from purgatory.

7th Hail Mary: for acceptance into the Confraternity.

8th Hail Mary: for the procession of the Rosary and for the oil lamp of the Rosary.

9th Hail Mary: for the devout recitation of the Rosary.

10th Hail Mary: for carrying the Rosary devoutly on one's person.

[41] *10th Our Father:* the Rosary is excellent because it was instituted for noble purposes that give much glory to God and are very salutary for souls.

1st Hail Mary: it inscribes us into this Confraternity to strengthen us in a wonderful way, joining us to many brothers and sisters.

2nd Hail Mary: to remind ourselves continually of the Mysteries of Jesus and Mary.

3rd Hail Mary: to praise God at every moment of the day and night and in every place in the world, something that is unattainable by ourselves alone.

4th Hail Mary: to thank our Lord for all the graces He grants us at every moment.

5th Hail Mary: to continually beg Him for pardon of our daily sins.

6th Hail Mary: to render our prayers more efficacious by uniting ourselves to others.

7th Hail Mary: to obtain mutual help at the hour of our death, which is very dangerous, difficult, and decisive.

8th Hail Mary: to be supported at the hour of judgment by as many advocates as there are members of the Confraternity.

9th Hail Mary: to be given relief after death and speedily set free from the pains of purgatory through the Masses and prayers offered by fellow members.

10th Hail Mary: to form an armada in battle array so as to destroy the reign of the devil and establish the Kingdom of Jesus Christ.

[42] *11th Our Father:* the Rosary is the great treasury of indulgences granted by Popes striving to outdo each other.

1st Hail Mary: plenary indulgence of the Stations of Rome and Jerusalem by receiving Communion on particular days.

2nd Hail Mary: plenary indulgence on the day of being inscribed into the Confraternity.

3rd Hail Mary: plenary indulgence at the point of death.

4th Hail Mary: indulgence for reciting the Rosary.

5th Hail Mary: indulgence for those who arrange for the recitation of the Rosary.

6th Hail Mary: plenary indulgence for those who receive Communion in the Church of the Rosary on the first Sunday of the month.

7th Hail Mary: indulgence for taking part in the procession.

8th Hail Mary: indulgence for those who have the Mass of the Rosary celebrated.

9th Hail Mary: indulgence for certain good works.

10th Hail Mary: indulgence for those who cannot visit the Church of the Rosary, nor receive Communion, nor take part in the procession.

[43] *12th Our Father:* the value of the Rosary is enhanced by the example of the Saints.

1st Hail Mary: St. Dominic, its author.

2nd Hail Mary: Blessed Alan de la Roche, its restorer.

3rd Hail Mary: the saintly Dominicans, its propagators.

4th Hail Mary: among the Popes: St. Pius V, Innocent III, and Boniface VIII, who had it embroidered in satin.

5th Hail Mary: among the Cardinals: St. Charles Borromeo.

6th Hail Mary: among the Bishops: St. Francis de Sales.

7th Hail Mary: among the Religious: St. Ignatius, St. Philip Neri, St. Felix of Cantalice.

8th Hail Mary: among the kings and queens: St. Louis; Philip I, King of Spain; Blanche, Queen of Castile.

9th Hail Mary: among the learned: St. Albert the Great, Navarre, etc.

10th Hail Mary: among the most devout: Sister Mary of the Incarnation, renowned holy woman of Rome.

[44] *13th Our Father:* the enemies of the Rosary who were overcome show us its glory.

1st Hail Mary: those who neglect it.

2nd Hail Mary: those who say it lukewarmly and distractedly.

3rd Hail Mary: those who say it hastily and out of habit.

4th Hail Mary: those who say it in unrepented mortal sin.

5th Hail Mary: those who say it out of hypocrisy and without any devotion.

6th Hail Mary: critics who seek to destroy it through trickery.

7th Hail Mary: the impious who attack it with their reasonings.

8th Hail Mary: the cowardly who, after embracing it, cast it aside.

9th Hail Mary: heretics who combat and slander it.

10th Hail Mary: the devils who hate it and seek to destroy it with a thousand schemes.

[45] *14th Our Father:* resolution of difficulties that heretics, libertines, the negligent, and the ignorant put forth to destroy it and to avoid saying it.

1st Hail Mary: **they object** . . . that the Rosary is a new practice.

2nd Hail Mary: . . . that it is an invention of Religious to obtain money.

3rd Hail Mary: . . . that it is a devotion of ignorant women who cannot read.

4th Hail Mary: . . . that it is a superstition because it is based on the repetition of prayers.

5th Hail Mary: . . . that it is better to recite the Penitential Psalms.

6th Hail Mary: . . . that it is better to meditate than to say the Rosary.

7th Hail Mary: . . . that the Rosary is too long and wearisome a prayer.

8th Hail Mary: . . . that we can be saved without saying the Rosary.

9th Hail Mary: . . . that if we neglect it, it is not true that we sin.

10th Hail Mary . . . that it is good act, but they do not have time to say it.

[46] *15th Our Father:* method for saying the Rosary well.

1st Hail Mary: it must be said with a right intention and with detachment from sin.

2nd Hail Mary: in a holy manner and without second intentions.

3rd Hail Mary: attentively and without voluntary distractions.

4th Hail Mary: slowly and with dignity, making good use of pauses.

5th Hail Mary: devoutly, with meditation on the Mysteries.

6th Hail Mary: in a self-composed manner while kneeling or standing.

7th Hail Mary: in its entirety and every day.

8th Hail Mary: in a low voice when it is said alone.

9th Hail Mary: publicly and in two choirs.

10th Hail Mary: with perseverance until death.

[47] *16th Our Father:* different methods for saying the Rosary.

1st Hail Mary: we can say the Rosary while thinking of the Mysteries and reciting simply the Our Father and the Hail Marys.

2nd Hail Mary: in every Mystery, we can add a word to the 10 Hail Marys.

3rd Hail Mary: at each decade, we can add a short offering.

4th Hail Mary: at each decade, we can add a longer offering.

5th Hail Mary: at every Hail Mary, we can add a particular intention.

6th Hail Mary: we can say it internally without pronouncing the words.

7th Hail Mary: at every Hail Mary, we can genuflect.

8th Hail Mary: at every Hail Mary, we can prostrate ourselves.

9th Hail Mary: at every Hail Mary, we can add some kind of penance.

10th Hail Mary: at every decade, we can commemorate the Saints and, in accord with the inspiration of the Holy Spirit, include a combination of some of the methods already mentioned.

APPENDICES

APPENDIX I

THE CONCLUDING MATERIAL OF
THE SECRET OF THE ROSARY

The Principal Rules of the Confraternity
of the Holy Rosary

[48] Members should:

(1) Have their names written in the Confraternity book and, if possible, go to Confession and Communion and say the Holy Rosary the same day that they are enrolled.

(2) Have a blessed Rosary.

(3) Say the Rosary every day or at least once a week.

(4) Whenever possible, go to Confession and Communion on the first Sunday of every month and take part in the procession of the Holy Rosary.

Remember that none of these rules binds under the pain of even venial sin.

The Power, Value, and Holiness
of the Rosary

A Revelation of the Blessed Virgin
to Blessed Alan de la Roche

[49] "Through the Rosary, many great sinners of both sexes became quickly converted to holy lives, lamenting their past sins and weeping deeply over them. Even children underwent incredible penances. In this way, devotion to my Son and to me flourished so greatly that it made one think Angels had descended on the earth. The Faith was also growing, to the point that many Catholics longed to shed their blood for it in the struggle against the heretics.

[50] "Thus, through the preaching of my very dear Dominic and through the power of the Rosary, the lands that were dominated by heretics were all brought under the Church. In virtue of the Rosary, people donated abundant alms, built churches and hospitals, led moral and law-abiding lives, and worked wonders. Great holiness and detachment from the world flourished as well as the honor of the Church, the justice of rulers, the peace of citizens, and the honesty of communities and families.

"Even more, workmen did not begin their labor until they had greeted me with my Psalter [i.e., Rosary], and they never retired for the night without having prayed in this way to me on their knees. If they chanced to recall that they had not paid me this tribute, they would rise, even in the middle of the night, and greet me with respect and remorse.

"The Rosary became so renowned that those who were devoted to it were always regarded as obviously being Confraternity members. If a person lived openly in sin or blasphemed, it was proverbial to say of him: 'This man cannot be a brother of St. Dominic.'

"I must not forget to mention the signs and wonders that I have wrought in various regions of the world through the Holy Rosary. I have shut down pestilences, put an end to horrible wars, and impeded the shedding of blood, and through my Rosary people have found the courage to flee temptation.

"Thus, the world rejoiced in my gifts, the Angels exulted because of your Psalters, the Blessed Trinity delighted in them, my Son found joy in them too, and I myself was happier than you can possibly imagine.

[51] "After the Holy Sacrifice of the Mass, there is nothing in the Church that I love so much as the Rosary.

"Having been strongly urged to do so by St. Dominic, all the brothers and sisters of his Order served my Son and me with great and indescribable devotion by continually reciting the Psalter of the Trinity [i.e., the Holy Rosary]. Every day each of them said at least one complete Rosary of 15 decades. If any of them failed to say it, they regarded their day as wasted.

"The brethren of St. Dominic had such great love for this devotion that it made them do everything better, and they would hurry to church or choir to sing the Office. If any of them were observed carrying out their duties carelessly, the others would say with assurance: 'Either you are not saying Mary's Psalter any more or else you are saying it badly.'"

The Dignity of the Hail Mary

[52] "The holy Angels in heaven greet the most Blessed Virgin with the Hail Mary, not with their voices but with spirits. They are aware that through it reparation was made for the fallen Angels' sin, God was made man, and the world was renewed" (Blessed Alan).

"I myself, recognizing the power of this annunciation of the Lord, used to recite it with much fervor. And, indeed, realizing my own human nature, I prayed to Mary in her supernatural life of grace and glory" (Blessed Alan).

"One night, when a woman Confraternity member had gone to bed, the Blessed Virgin appeared to her and said: 'My daughter, do not be afraid of me. I am your loving Mother whom you praise so faithfully every day. Stand fast and persevere. I want you to know that the Angelic Salutation gives me so much joy that no one could ever really explain it' " (William Pepin, in *The Golden Rosary,* Sermon 47).

[53] This is corroborated by a vision of St. Gertrude. In her *Revelations* (bk. IV, ch. 11), we read: "On the morning of a feast of the Annunciation of the Blessed Virgin Mary, while the Hail Mary was being sung in the monastery where Gertrude lived, the Saint saw three streams that flowed, the first from the Father, the second from the Son, and the third from the Holy Spirit, and greatly filled the heart of the Virgin Mother.

"Then from this heart, they returned impetuously to their source. By this influence of the Blessed

Trinity, St. Gertrude learned that Mary was adorned with the gift of being the most powerful after God the Father, the most wise after God the Son, and the most loving after God the Holy Spirit.

"On that occasion, the Saint also learned that whenever the faithful recite the Angelic Salutation the three mysterious streams surround the Blessed Virgin with impetuosity and abundance. They rush into her heart, inundating her with sweetness and then return to God's bosom.

"Part of this abundance of joy is shared by the Saints and Angels in heaven and by all on earth who say the Angelic Salutation, which renews everything good in the children of God."

[54] This is what the Blessed Virgin herself said in a vision to St. Mechtilde:"Never has anyone composed anything more beautiful than the Hail Mary. And it is not possible to greet me in a sweeter fashion than with these respectful words with which God Himself chose to greet me."

Speaking of a vision of the Blessed Virgin to one of her devotees, Blessed Denis the Carthusian said: "Here emblazoned on my cloak are all the Angelic Salutations that you have presented to me. When this part of my cloak is full of Hail Marys, I shall take you into the Kingdom of my Beloved Son."

Richard of St. Laurence said: "We should greet the most Blessed Virgin with our hearts, our lips, and our deeds, so that she will not be able to say to us:'These people honor me with their lips, but their hearts are far from me.'"

[55] * Richard of St. Laurence gives the reasons why it is good to say a Hail Mary at the beginning of a sermon:

(1) *To imitate the example of the Archangel.* The Church Militant imitates insofar as possible the conduct of St. Gabriel who respectfully greeted the Blessed Virgin with "Hail Mary" before telling her the Good News with the words: "Behold, you shall conceive in your womb and bring forth a Son." Accordingly, the Church greets Mary before proclaiming the Gospel.

(2) *To show that the preacher acts in the place of the Angel.* In order for the hearers to bring forth Christ with faith, they need to obtain this grace from the Blessed Virgin, who first brought Him forth. In this way, they will become mothers of the Word of God. Without Mary, they cannot bring forth Christ.

(3) *To obtain the help of the Blessed Virgin.* In this respect, the Gospel shows the effectiveness of the Angelic Salutation.

(4) *To avoid the great dangers involved in preaching.* Mary, the Illuminatrix, enlighten preachers.

(5) *To enable the hearers, after Mary's example, to listen more attentively.* In this way, they remember the Word of God with greater care.

(6) *To drive away the devil, who is the enemy of the human race and of the preaching of the Gospel.*

---

* All of number 55 is quoted by St. Louis from a book of sermons on the Litany of Loreto by Justin Mieckovic, O.P.

For, according to the word of Christ, we must remain watchful that the devil will not take the word of Christ "away from people's hearts and prevent them from believing and being saved" (Luke 8:12).

[56] In his first sermon on the Holy Rosary, Clement Losow said:

"After St. Dominic had gone to heaven, devotion to the Rosary began to wane until it was nearly dead. It was then that a frightful epidemic broke out and started to devastate several parts of the country. Not knowing what to do, the people sought the advice of a saintly hermit who lived in the desert in great austerity, and they begged him to intercede with God for them. The holy man had recourse to the Mother of God and implored her, as Advocate of Sinners, to come to their aid.

"The Blessed Virgin then appeared to the holy man and said: 'These people have stopped singing my praises; that is why they have been visited with such a scourge. If they return to the ancient devotion of the Rosary, they will once again enjoy my protection. I will provide for their salvation if they will honor me by saying the Rosary, for this Psalter is very pleasing to me.'

"Accordingly, the people carried out Mary's request. They made themselves Rosaries and started saying them with all their hearts."

APPENDIX II

APPENDIX II*

THE NEW LUMINOUS MYSTERIES
OF THE ROSARY

O_N October 16, 2002, Pope John Paul II issued an Apostolic Letter, entitled *The Rosary of the Blessed Virgin Mary,* encouraging all Catholics to recite the Rosary. In it the Pope said:**

"The Rosary, though clearly Marian in character, is at heart a Christocentric prayer. In the sobriety of its elements, it has all the *depth of the Gospel message in its entirety,* of which it can be said to be a compendium.

"It is an echo of the prayer of Mary, her perennial *Magnificat* for the work of the redemptive Incarnation which began in her virginal womb. With the Rosary, the Christian people *sits at the school of Mary* and is led to contemplate the beauty on the face of Christ and to experience the depths of His love. Through the Rosary the faithful receive abundant grace, as though from the very hands of the Mother of the Redeemer. . . .

"There are some who think that the centrality of the Liturgy, rightly stressed by the Second Vatican Ecumenical Council, necessarily entails giving lesser importance to the Rosary. Yet, as Pope Paul VI made clear, not only does this prayer not conflict

---

* We are adding this appendix to provide our readers with the new Luminous Mysteries of the Rosary, suggested by Pope John Paul II on October 16, 2002. To complete the picture we are also including a sample of how these Mysteries can be said in Methods I to IV of St. Louis de Montfort.

** See nos. 1, 4, 5, 19 of the Letter.

with the Liturgy, *[the Rosary] sustains [the Liturgy]*, since it serves as an excellent introduction and a faithful echo of the Liturgy, enabling people to participate fully and interiorly in it and to reap its fruits in their daily lives. . . .

"But the most important reason for strongly encouraging the practice of the Rosary is that it represents a most effective means of fostering among the faithful that *commitment to the contemplation of the Christian Mystery* which I have proposed in the Apostolic Letter *On the Threshold of the New Millennium* as a genuine 'training in holiness': 'What is needed is a Christian life distinguished above all in the *art of prayer.*'

"Inasmuch as contemporary culture, even amid so many indications to the contrary, has witnessed the flowering of a new call for spirituality, due also to the influence of other religions, it is more urgent than ever that our Christian communities should become 'genuine schools of prayer.'"

At the same time, the Pope also suggested five new Mysteries that might supplement the meditation on the traditional Joyful, Sorrowful, and Glorious Mysteries of the Rosary. The new Mysteries, called the Luminous Mysteries (or Mysteries of Light), are intended to offer contemplation on important parts of Christ's Public Life in addition to the contemplation on His Childhood, His Sufferings, and His Risen Life offered by the traditional Mysteries:

"Of the many Mysteries of Christ's life, only a few are indicated by the Rosary in the form that has become generally established with the seal of the Church's approval. . . .

"I believe, however, that to bring out fully the Christological depth of the Rosary it would be suitable to make an addition to the traditional pattern which, while left to the freedom of individuals and communities, could broaden it to include *the Mysteries of Christ's Public Ministry between His Baptism and His Passion.*

"In the course of those Mysteries we contemplate important aspects of the person of Christ as the definitive revelation of God. Declared the beloved Son of the Father at the Baptism in the Jordan, Christ is the One Who announces the coming of the Kingdom, bears witness to it in His works, and proclaims its demands. It is during the years of his Public Ministry that the *Mystery of Christ is most evidently a Mystery of Light:* 'While I am in the world, I am the light of the world' (John 9:5).

"Consequently . . . it is fitting to add, following reflection on the Incarnation and the Hidden Life of Christ *(the Joyful Mysteries)* and before focusing on the sufferings of His Passion *(the Sorrowful Mysteries)* and the triumph of His Resurrection *(the Glorious Mysteries),* a meditation on *certain particularly significant moments in His Public Ministry (the Luminous Mysteries).*"

The Pope assigned these new Mysteries to Thursday while transferring the Joyful Mysteries—normally said on that day—to Saturday (the traditional day for honoring Mary) because of the special Marian presence in them.

First Method of Praying the
Luminous Mysteries

For introduction, see p. 171.

1st Decade: Lord Jesus, we offer You this first decade in honor of Your Baptism, and we ask of You, through this Mystery and through the intercession of Your Holy Mother, *the grace to fulfill our Baptismal promises.*

1 Our Father, 10 Hail Marys, 1 Glory Be to the Father . . .

May the grace of the Mystery of the Baptism of Jesus come down into my soul and make it regain its Baptismal purity.

2nd Decade: Lord Jesus, we offer You this second decade in honor of Your Self-Manifestation at the Wedding Feast of Cana, and we ask of You, through this Mystery and through the intercession of Your Holy Mother, *the willingness to do whatever You say.*

1 Our Father, 10 Hail Marys, 1 Glory Be to the Father . . .

May the grace of the Mystery of the Self-Manifestation of Jesus come down into my soul and make it do whatever He tells me.

3rd Decade: Lord Jesus, we offer You this third decade in honor of the Mystery of Your Proclamation of the Kingdom of God, and we ask of You, through this Mystery and through the intercession of Your Holy Mother, *forgiveness for our sins.*

1 Our Father, 10 Hail Marys, 1 Glory Be to the Father . . .

May the grace of the Mystery of Christ's Proclamation of the Kingdom of God come down into my soul and take away my sins.

4th Decade: Lord Jesus, we offer You this fourth decade in honor of Your Transfiguration, and we ask of You, through this Mystery and through the intercession of Your Holy Mother, *the firm desire to become new persons.*

1 Our Father, 10 Hail Marys, 1 Glory Be to the Father . . .

May the grace of the Mystery of the Transfiguration come down into my soul and make me a new person in Christ.

5th Decade: Lord Jesus, we offer You this fifth decade in honor of the Mystery of the Institution of the Eucharist, and we ask of You, through this Mystery and through the intercession of Your Holy Mother, *the desire to achieve active participation at every Mass.*

1 Our Father, 10 Hail Marys, 1 Glory Be to the Father . . .

May the grace of the Mystery of Christ's Institution of the Eucharist come down into my soul and inspire me to strive for active participation at every Mass.

Second Method of Praying the Luminous Mysteries

For Introduction, see p. 178.

1st decade: . . . and blessed is the fruit of your womb, "Jesus in His Baptism."

2nd decade: . . . and blessed is the fruit of your

womb, "Jesus in His Self-Manifestation at Cana."

3rd decade: . . . and blessed is the fruit of your womb, "Jesus proclaiming the kingdom of God."

4th decade: . . . and blessed is the fruit of your womb, "Jesus in His Transfiguration."

5th decade: . . . and blessed is the fruit of your womb, "Jesus instituting the Eucharist."

At the end of these Mysteries, we say:

May the grace of the Luminous Mysteries come down into our souls and make us proclaim Your Kingdom.

Third Method of Praying the Luminous Mysteries

For all intents and purposes, this is the same as the First Method, p. 171, except for the fact that the request for the grace of the Mystery, which ends every decade, is placed in the plural.

Fourth Method of Praying the Luminous Mysteries

For Introduction, see p. 191.

To use this method entails replacing St. Louis's Fifth Joyful Mystery with the one below.

The Finding of Jesus in the Temple

Our Father: the unfathomable holiness of God.

1st Hail Mary: to honor Christ's Hidden Life at Nazareth filled with hard work and obedience.

2nd Hail Mary: His preaching and His Finding among the Doctors in the Temple.

3rd Hail Mary: His obedience to His parents.

4th Hail Mary: His growth in knowledge.

5th Hail Mary: His advance in understanding the Old Testament.

6th Hail Mary: His increased consciousness of His special relationship with His Father in heaven.

7th Hail Mary: His spiritual growth through private prayer and the worship in the Temple.

8th Hail Mary: His aid given to his foster father until St. Joseph's death.

9th Hail Mary: His tender care for Mary in her widowhood.

10th Hail Mary: His departure from home to begin His Public Life.

1. The Baptism of Jesus

Our Father: God's eternal plan of salvation.

1st Hail Mary: to honor Jesus for His forty days of fasting and prayer in the desert.

2nd Hail Mary: His victory over Satan's temptations.

3rd Hail Mary: the baptism of repentance preached by St. John the Baptist at the Jordan.

4th Hail Mary: Jesus' arrival to be baptized by St. John and fulfill all justice.

5th Hail Mary: His Baptism at the hands of St. John.

6th Hail Mary: the coming of the Holy Spirit upon Him.

7th Hail Mary: the Father's identification of Him as the Servant of the Lord.

8th Hail Mary: His wondrous preaching.

9th Hail Mary: His stupendous miracles.

10th Hail Mary: the selection of the Twelve Apostles and the power given them.

2. Christ's Self-Manifestation at Cana

Our Father: God's choice of Mary as the first believer and as the Associate of Jesus.

1st Hail Mary: to honor Jesus in the confirmation of His saving mission.

2nd Hail Mary: Jesus' presence at a wedding together with His Apostles and Mary.

3rd Hail Mary: Mary's request for aid when the wine runs out.

4th Hail Mary: Jesus' answer that His hour has not yet come.

5th Hail Mary: Mary's words to the servants: "Do whatever He tells you."

6th Hail Mary: Jesus' instructions to the servants to fill six stone water jars with water.

7th Hail Mary: Jesus' instructions to take some out and bring it to the chief steward.

8th Hail Mary: the chief steward's finding that the jars contained choice wine.

9th Hail Mary: this first of Jesus' signs revealed His glory.

10th Hail Mary: the belief of His disciples in Jesus.

3. Christ's Proclamation of the Kingdom of God

Our Father: the Beatitudes: Magna Carta of the Kingdom.

1st Hail Mary: to honor Jesus as the herald of God's Kingdom.

2nd Hail Mary: time for repentance and belief in the Gospel.

3rd Hail Mary: the poor in spirit will attain the Kingdom.

4th Hail Mary: those who mourn will be comforted.

5th Hail Mary: the meek will inherit the earth.

6th Hail Mary: those who hunger and thirst for justice will have their fill.

7th Hail Mary: the merciful will obtain mercy.

8th Hail Mary: the pure of heart will see God.

9th Hail Mary: the peacemakers will be called children of God.

10th Hail Mary: those who are persecuted in the cause of justice will inherit the Kingdom.

4. The Transfiguration of Our Lord

Our Father: vision of Jesus in glory.

1st Hail Mary: to honor Jesus, the Teacher of the Law and the Prophets.

2nd Hail Mary: the journey of Jesus with Sts. Peter, John, and James to a high mountain.

3rd Hail Mary: the Transfiguration of Jesus—His face shining like the sun and His clothes becoming dazzling white.

4th Hail Mary: the appearance of Moses (symbolizing the Law) and Elijah (symbolizing the Prophets) speaking with Him.

5th Hail Mary: Peter's words: "It is good for us to be here."

6th Hail Mary: the shadow cast upon them by a bright cloud.

7th Hail Mary: the words of the voice from the cloud: "This is My Beloved Son, with Whom I am well pleased. Listen to Him."

8th Hail Mary: the fear of the Apostles.

9th Hail Mary: Christ's words: "Stand up and do not be frightened."

10th Hail Mary: Raising their eyes, the Apostles saw only Jesus.

5. Christ's Institution of the Eucharist

Our Father: God's desire to remain among human beings.

1st Hail Mary: to honor Jesus in His Sacramental Presence.

2nd Hail Mary: preparations for the Passover.

3rd Hail Mary: Jesus at table with the Apostles.

4th Hail Mary: "I have eagerly desired to eat this Passover with you before I suffer."

5th Hail Mary: "I shall never eat it again until it is fulfilled in the Kingdom of God."

6th Hail Mary: "Take this cup and divide it among yourselves."

7th Hail Mary: "I will not drink of the fruit of the vine until the Kingdom of God comes."

8th Hail Mary: "This is My Body, which will be given for you."

9th Hail Mary: "Do this in memory of Me."

10th Hail Mary: He did the same with the cup after supper, saying: "This cup is the New Covenant in My Blood, which will be poured out for you."

APPENDIX III

The Rosary Indulgences in Effect Today*

A *plenary indulgence* is granted when the rosary is recited in a church or oratory or when it is recited in a family, a religious community, or a pious association. A *partial indulgence* is granted for its recitation in all other circumstances.

(The rosary is a prayer formula divided into fifteen decades of Hail Mary's with the *Lord's Prayer* separating each of these decades. During each of these decades we recall in devout meditation the mysteries of our redemption.)

It has become customary to call but five such decades the "rosary" also. Concerning this customary usage then, the following norms are given as regards a plenary indulgence.

1. The recitation of a third of the rosary is sufficient for obtaining the plenary indulgence, but these five decades must be recited without interruption.

2. Devout meditation on the mysteries is to be added to the vocal prayer.

3. In its public recitation the mysteries must be announced in accord with approved local custom, but in its private recitation it is sufficient for the

---

* Excerpted from *The Handbook of Indulgences* (no. 48), Authorized English Edition (© 1991 by Catholic Book Publishing Co.), published by authority of the Bishops' Committee on the Liturgy, National Conference of Catholic Bishops.

Christian faithful simply to join meditation on the mysteries to the vocal prayer.

4. In the Eastern Churches where recitation of the Marian rosary as a devotional practice is not found, the patriarchs can establish other prayers in honor of the blessed Virgin Mary which will have the same indulgences as those attached to the rosary, (e.g., in the Byzantine churches, the Akathist hymn, or the office *Paraclisis.)*